PERSEVERANCE IN TRIALS

PERSEVERANCE IN TRIALS

Reflections on Job

Cardinal Carlo Maria Martini
Archbishop of Milan

Translated
by
Matthew J. O'Connell

A Liturgical Press Book

 THE LITURGICAL PRESS
Collegeville, Minnesota

Cover design by Mary Jo Pauly

Avete Perseverato con me nelle mie Prove © copyright by Edizioni Piemme
S.p.A., Via del Carmine 5, 15033 Casale Monferrato (AL), Italy.

1   2   3   4   5   6   7   8   9

Library of Congress Cataloging-in-Publication Data

Martini, Carlo M.
    [Avete persevarato con me nelle mie prove. English]
    Perseverance in trials : reflections on Job / Carlo Maria Martini.
      p. cm.
    Includes index.
    ISBN 0-8146-2060-4
    1. Bible. O.T. Job—Meditations. 2. Bible. O.T. Job—
Criticism, interpretation, etc. I. Title.
BS1415.4.M3713 1992
269'.692—dc20   92-19276
                                       CIP

This retreat was preached to a group of priests at Rho, Italy,
August 21–25, 1989.

Contents

Preface

''You have stood by me in my trials'' is the title of a retreat given by Cardinal Carlo Maria Martini, Archbishop of Milan, to a group of priests, chiefly from the diocese of St. Ambrose.

The consoling words which Jesus speaks to his disciples just before his passion are a reminder to us that Christian life, like the life of human beings generally, is marked by trials. For this reason, the author has chosen the Book of Job as a primary text for reflection, although other passages of the Old and New Testaments are also offered for meditation.

The story of this mysterious man, who did not belong to the chosen people but lived in a distant land, was perhaps being passed from mouth to mouth among the wise men of the East as early as the end of the second millennium B.C. It was written down in Hebrew only a good deal later. Job, who was an upright man and regarded himself as such, is tested and deprived of everything. The Jews exiled in Babylonia had likewise lost everything; this tested their faith in the justice of God, from whom they had thought they could claim certain rights. As they tried to understand the hidden meaning of the suffering that weighed upon them despite their right behavior before God, they probably read and sang the lamentations of Job. Can a human being require God to account for his actions? The poet counters with his own view: we must not demand that God give his reasons, but rather believe in his justice and incomprehensible wisdom.

In comments marked by spiritual and pastoral depth, the cardinal dwells on certain passages of Job that help to shed light on the meaning of the mystery of the human person and the mystery of God. He notes that in the dialogue between Satan and God in the first two chapters "the issue takes the form of a . . . wager laid on a human being: Is any human action completely selfless?" The problem of Job is first and foremost a problem of faith; bargaining has no place in the life of faith because the sublimity of faith calls for the response of selfless devotion. Job has indeed not committed any of the sins of which his friends accuse him; he has, however, committed the supreme sin of a religious person: he has passed judgment on God. The archbishop's reflections challenge us to examine the quality of our faith, the character of our prayer as the submission of our whole being to the ineffable mystery of God, and our obedience of mind. In the end, as the unusual comparison of Job with the Song of Songs brings out, Job's quest proves to be a problem of love.

If the reading of this book is to be fully fruitful, the reader must bring to it a spiritual commitment that flees mediocrity and sets the soul thirsting for God. Worth noting here is the aim the archbishop assigns to this retreat: a new conversion to the spirit of prayer. When read in an atmosphere of prayer, these pages become a source of light, nourishment, strength, incentive, and consolation.

They point out to us, among other things, that all human beings of good will are already searching for God; they are confronted with the way in which the Almighty directs his universe, and they experience within themselves the criticism which their consciences level at their actions.

These pages teach us also to extricate the reality of God from the limitations we place on it and from our morality insofar as this is seen as a source of self-justification. For the object of faith is primarily the incomprehensible divine love that anticipates and transcends us. From this love, in which Christians believe once they have contemplated the sign of the Crucified, we can receive the power to love selflessly, to love even in trial and tribulation. These pages exhort us, therefore, to grow in the faith that loves and hopes, and to be eager for a relationship with the Lord in which our full freedom truly enters into play.

The God who gives himself to us in the covenant desires only our heartfelt love and devotion.

ONE

Introduction to the Retreat

"We thank you, Father, for calling us together from all parts of the diocese and even from other parts of Italy to listen to your word, to receive the gift of your Son's love and mercy, to be strengthened and consoled interiorly by the Holy Spirit who is love and peace.

"We ask you to pour out your Spirit of love and peace abundantly on each of us during these days. I myself thank you for what I experienced at Santiago de Compostella in the company of the Pope and hundreds of thousands of young people; for the faith and hope we shared with one another, for the gifts given us as we looked to the future of the Church: a future so richly endowed with various strengths, with the spirit of sacrifice, with courage and joy.

"Grant that we may be able to serve these young people who ask and expect much of us.

"Here in your presence, Father, we are conscious of our poverty and our ignorance of what to say or think, but we also have confidence that any adequacy, any ability we may have comes from you through the grace of the Holy Spirit and the grace bestowed by the ministry of the new covenant. Virgin Mary, Mother of Jesus and our Mother, lead us through this retreat. You endured many trials and your soul was pierced by a sword: grant that we may grasp the meaning of the trials which we, as well as the human race and the Church, are experiencing."

Renewing the Spirit of Prayer

The basic purpose of a retreat is to seek conversion, to ask God to change us for the better.

Among the many possible areas for conversion of life—areas which each of us can list for himself—I want to emphasize the necessity of renewing the spirit of prayer. Our need of this renewal is very great, for during the course of the year the sheer multiplicity of the tasks before us ends up attenuating that spirit.

I think it important for us to recover it during these days, and this in three areas:

• the time given to prayer, which can well be longer;

• good habits, which tend to unravel and which we can bring under our renewed control in the course of each day here;

• our manner of praying, which should be marked by three attitudes. First of all, devotion, that is, a respect for God that shows itself in our words, in our bodily postures, in attentiveness and silence. Next, the submission of our entire being to the mystery of God, or loving reverence. Finally, affectivity, for prayer is an activity involving the affections. It may be that due to the difficult circumstances of our life the affections remain in the background or even in the unconscious; during these days we should bring them to the forefront so that we may learn to resist the indifferentism around us. Without a deep, affective sense of God in prayer it is in fact almost impossible to combat successfully the atheism that surrounds us here in the West.

For myself, I shall endeavor to promote this reconversion to the spirit of prayer by suggesting some thoughts on a subject derived from words of Jesus at the Last Supper: "You are those who have stood by me in my trials" (Lk 22:28).

The Theme of the Retreat

This is a wonderful statement of Jesus, and if at the end of our lives we hear it said to us: "You are one who has stood by me in my trials," we shall be filled with joy. It is worth noting that this statement of Jesus is made just after the apostles have been disputing among themselves: "A dispute also arose among them as to which one of them was to be regarded as the greatest" (Lk 22:24).

Here, then, is a squabble that brings to light the ambitions, the tensions, the little envies existing within the group of disciples. Jesus takes advantage of it to teach that whoever wants to be greatest must serve, and then he immediately goes on to say: "You are those who have stood by me in my trials." He is not under the illusion that the Twelve have reached a high degree of holiness; he does, however, know that there can be great fidelity even where there is failure, weakness, and pettiness.

By way of introduction to subsequent meditations I invite you to reflect on the various elements in the gospel statement: trials, perseverance in trials, "my" trials, perseverance "with me."

1. The Greek word *peirasmos* occurs rather frequently in the scriptures.

Its first meaning is "a probing," "a trying": the endeavor to determine what someone's capabilities are, how faithful, how persevering, how strong someone is.

The Bible then adds two further meanings to this original one: a) temptation, which is an incitement to sin by a malignant power or, in any case, by the harmful inclinations arising from the evil in the world. The word signifies the temptations, in the true and proper sense, that are interwoven with human life; b) trial or testing; it is to this that Jesus refers, and it can come from God. Jesus is alluding to the situations of affliction and trouble which we often encounter. These make up, in part, the journey of the word within us, its insertion into the earth of the human heart. Thus in the parable of the sower we read, of the seeds that fall upon rock: "The ones on the rock are those who, when they hear the word, receive it with joy. But these have no root; they believe only for a while and in a time of testing fall away'' (Lk 8:13).

Thus, when the word enters the human heart, it is subjected to testing. Matthew the evangelist tells us some of the ways in which it is tested: "As for what was sown on rocky ground, this is the one who hears the word and immediately receives it with joy; yet such a person has no root, but endures only for a while, and when trouble or persecution arises on account of the word, that person immediately falls away" (Mt 13:20-21).

Trial, temptation, trouble, or whatever we choose to call it, is an ordinary and recurring event in human life on earth and especially in the lives of the "just," that is, those who strive to be faithful to God and seek to walk in his ways.

The Book of Job expresses this thought in a poetic manner, especially when Job says: "Do not human beings have a hard service on earth?" (Jb 7:1). The note in *The New Jerusalem Bible* explains that the word here translated as "hard service" refers to military service, which involves both fighting and forced labor. The Greek version of the Old Testament (the Septuagint) translates the Hebrew word as "trial," referring to the trials that mark human life. The Vulgate, for its part, has the familiar sentence: "The life of man upon earth is a warfare (*militia est vita hominis super terram*)," which is taken up by *The Imitation of Christ*, Book I, Chapter 13, "On Resisting Temptation." This well-known chapter begins: "As long as our life in this world lasts, we cannot be free of trials and temptations. Therefore is it written in the Book of Job: 'The life of man upon earth is a temptation.'"

Job continues:

> and are not their days like the days of a laborer?
> Like a slave who longs for the shadow,
>   and like laborers who look for their wages,
> so I am allotted months of emptiness,
>   and nights of misery are apportioned to me.
> When I lie down I say, "When shall I rise?"
>   But the night is long,

and I am full of tossing until dawn.
My flesh is clothed with worms and dirt;
   my skin hardens, then breaks out again.
My days are swifter than a weaver's shuttle,
   and come to their end without hope.
Remember that my life is but a breath (7:1-7a)

The New Jerusalem Bible says in a note: ''Accepting the human lot of suffering and death, Job breaks momentarily into prayer asking God for a few moments of peace before he dies'' (p. 765).

The Old Testament passage uses very concrete language in describing human life as a testing.

2. Referring to this testing or trial, Jesus says to his disciples: ''You are those who *have stood by* me.'' The Greek says, more simply, ''have remained''; that is: you are the ones who have not gone away. Jesus is praising them: You suffered enough that you might well have gone away, but you did not do so.

We are reminded of John 6:67-68, where Jesus says: ''Do you also wish to go away?'' and Peter answers: ''Lord, to whom can we go?'' Jesus bears witness that the apostles stayed until the end; they stood by him and did not abandon him.

The idea of perseverance occurs often in the scriptures and is expressed in various ways. For example: ''to keep the word'' implies lasting and stubborn patience: ''But as for that [seed] in the good soil, these are the ones who, when they hear the word, hold it fast in an honest and good heart, and bear fruit with patient endurance'' (Lk 8:15). When situations test us we face up to them by perseverance and persistence, by endurance, by keeping the word. Trials tend to make us turn back; they persuade us to lose heart. The direct opposite is not necessarily immediate victory; rather it is the endurance that enables us to stand firm and strong. John the evangelist uses a very simple verb: *menein* (''remain'' or ''abide''), which in context carries the same overtones. ''If you abide in me,'' Jesus says, ''and my words abide in you, ask for whatever you wish, and it will be done for you'' (Jn 15:7). ''Abiding in Jesus'' is the way to meet trials and tests.

3. ''You have stood by me in *my* trials,'' not just ''in trials'' generally.

This personal reference gives our human life an entirely new aspect.

We ask ourselves: What are the trials of Jesus?

• As a matter of fact, the gospel provides little information on this point, but what it does say is enough to show that Jesus too was tempted and tried.

''The Spirit immediately drove him out into the wilderness. He was in the wilderness forty days, tempted by Satan'': thus does Mark begin his account of the Lord's public life (Mk 1:12-13). The fact that the writer puts the reference to testing at the very beginning shows that Jesus was not tempted only on one occasion but that his entire life was lived under the sign of trials.

The Letter to the Hebrews offers a further insight: ''We do not have a high priest who is unable to sympathize with our weaknesses, but we have one who in every respect has been tested, as we are, yet without sin'' (Heb 4:15). ''In every respect'': therefore in the many difficult, burdensome, laborious, and repugnant aspects of concrete life through which Jesus passed and which he shared with the Twelve.

• But the expression ''my trials'' cannot be limited to the historical circumstances of Jesus of Nazareth. He speaks of himself as the Messiah, as one who makes his own the life of the entire people of God and the journey of this people to the Father. We must therefore take the words as referring to the messianic trials, the trials of the kingdom. The apostles shared in these trials; they were sifted, winnowed, ground down. Many of the trials we believers face come from the concrete situations in the social and historical setting that is ours, namely, the Catholic Church with its problems, its labors, its afflictions and troubles. These are the trials of Jesus as head of the messianic people.

• There is a further step to be taken. From the moment when Jesus becomes Son of Man, he makes his own and experiences in himself the trials of every man and woman on earth. He is the head of the human race, and his trials expand to embrace those of the vast multitude of individuals who have inhabited, now inhabit, and will inhabit the earth.

As we grow in experience of life, we grow also in our share in these trials, for we have a better knowledge of the Church and human beings; we extend the range of our friendships to embrace a larger number of individuals and we suffer with them.

Each of us makes the trials of Lebanon our own, because the Pope feels them; we read the newpapers, we watch television, we know individuals from that country.

The trials of China, too, are ours; the trials of poverty-stricken India; the trials of the peoples of Latin America and Africa, with their terrible misery and hunger. Ours are the trials of Israel, the Jewish people, the chosen people, with all the troubles they face and the problems they have in engaging in dialogue.

All this weighs upon us; at times it angers and disturbs us because it winnows our faith, our hope, our love, our patience, our endurance, our sense of our limitations. Yet these are the trials which Jesus calls "my trials."

Then, too, of course, each of us experiences the trials of those entrusted to us: the people of the parish, the young, those toward whom we have specific pastoral obligations. Each of us is in some measure overwhelmed by the sufferings of our own people, our colleagues, and all whom we love.

All these are the trials of Jesus the Messiah, the Son of Man, the head of the messianic people, and the head of the human race. We share in them in reality and not just in imagination, and we share closely in them.

4. "You have stood *by me* in my trials." The trials in question are not merely objective, as if they were boulders or waves pouring down on us. When Jesus adds "by me," he gives

these trials a different "taste," as it were; he introduces and emphasizes an affective, personal, intimate dimension. We suffer them with him, out of love for him, in close relationship with him. He asks us to approach them in this way so that we may better identify and understand them, for it is indeed important that we manage to confront trials directly.

We often feel oppressed, exhausted, frustrated by something vague about our trials. The Lord urges us to give our troubles a name, list them, and then learn how to face them with him. For it is a basic element in human and Christian wisdom that we should understand the usefulness of trials and weather them faithfully.

In addition, the more we love, and the more we serve and make ourselves available, the greater these trials are.

If, on the other hand, we lock ourselves up in our own little world, if we become misanthropes, if we do not emerge from our self-centeredness, we shall experience only the trial of personal frustration.

St. James the Apostle begins his letter with this exhortation: "My brothers and sisters, whenever you face trials of any kind, consider it nothing but joy, because you know that the testing of your faith produces endurance; and let endurance have its full effect, so that you may be mature and complete, lacking in nothing" (Jas 1:2). Further on, he adds: "Blessed is anyone who endures temptation. Such a one has stood the test and will receive the crown of life that the Lord has promised to those who love him" (1:12). This summation of human life by St. James expresses the highest wisdom of the entire New Testament.

The Apocalypse, which is the supreme document about Christians enduring trials, has this to say on the subject: "Because you have kept my word of patient endurance, I will keep you from the hour of trial that is coming on the whole world to test the inhabitants of the earth" (Rv 3:10). The author is referring to the idea of cosmic, universal trial—an idea that keeps cropping up in our own time, especially in apocalyptic predictions. The prayer we recite daily alludes perhaps to such a trial: "Lead us not into temptation," that is, do not let us succumb in the great trial.

We must, however, be aware of the nature of this universal, cosmic trial in which we are in fact immersed and of which we are often not conscious, even though it embraces our real life in its totality.

The Book of Job

The theme of the retreat thus has to do with something that is a constant element of our life but that should not sadden us. I will go further: Only by facing trials in a certain way shall we be assured of a peaceful life. It is not the elimination of trials but the acceptance of them that makes Christian joy unique.

During these days we want to reflect in the presence of Jesus, who says to each of us: "You are one who desires to stand by me in my trials; I want to help you, to give you a hand; I urge you to pray and meditate, to face up to your trials, to give them a distinct name, thus removing all vagueness from them. And then I want to help you accept them with love and to embrace them as I embraced the cross."

"Lord, grant that we may share your courageous outlook; that we may enter into your truth and so be able to experience the joy reserved for those who with high hearts face up to life as a trial."

Having looked through the pages of scripture that refer to the theme of struggle, trial, and temptation, I shall dwell especially on the Book of Job, the book that deals with the trials to which human beings are subject. I suggest, therefore, that you read through the book, since I shall not be able to comment on the entire text.

I ask you, in addition, to read once again at least some chapters of *The Imitation of Christ*, a somewhat forgotten book that nonetheless conveys a profound understanding of human life as a trial. It is a book rich in wisdom, balance, and serenity, for its author had a strong sense of the temptations and trials that mark human existence. The Fathers who commented on the Book of Job had the same sense; for example, St. Gregory the Great, an outstanding Pope who saw all of life as a trial and found a great deal of strength in meditating on and explaining this book of the scriptures.

Let us be guided, then, by these teachers of the faith, and, as we reflect on the words of Jesus in the Gospel of Luke, let us pray:

"Lord, grant that I may see my own trials clearly. Grant that I may learn how to face up to them and be able to overcome those of my people, so that together we may consciously share in the trials of the whole Church, of our diocese, and of the entire human race at this critical moment in world history."

TWO

Introduction to the Mystery of Trials

"Grant, O Lord, that we may let ourselves face the reality of trials in our lives; they are not simply a fact but a mystery, for it is through them that we grasp an aspect of the experiential historical contingency that marks our being, and at the same time grasp something of you. We desire to know you and to enter with heart and mind into your ineffable mystery. Therefore, Father, grant that in some small degree we may also contemplate your mystery through the experience of trials."

I suggest as a subject for this opening meditation the first two chapters of the Book of Job, which form a prose introduction to the poem proper.

First, let us do a summary reading of these chapters and then ask ourselves some questions.

For some time now I have wanted to reflect on Job during a retreat. At the same time, however, I have been hesitant to do so, because this fascinating book is also a very difficult one. St. Jerome compares it to an eel: the harder we try to lay hold of it, the more it eludes us.

In the end, I decided to review during these days at least some pages that will help us open somewhat the door to this mysterious document with its many puzzles: philological, historical, literary, and interpretative.

The Story in the Prologue of Job

There are three main characters in the story:

The first is Job, who lived in the land of Uz and therefore outside the boundaries of Israel. He was "blameless and upright, one who feared God and turned away from evil" (1:1). He was also a rich man: "There were born to him seven sons and three daughters. He had seven thousand sheep, three thousand camels, five hundred yoke of oxen, five hundred donkeys, and very many servants; so that this man was the greatest of all the people of the East" (1:2-3).

The second main character of the Prologue is Satan, the Accuser, a mysterious personage who turns up at the court of God and throws a negative light on the actions of human beings. He asks that Job be tested.

The third personage in the drama is God, who from his court on high follows the doings of human beings and in some manner has them present before his eyes.

The story includes two phases or trials:

First, Job is tested in his possessions. "A messenger came to Job and said, 'The oxen were plowing and the donkeys were feeding beside them, and the Sabeans fell on them and carried them off, and killed the servants with the edge of the sword: I alone have escaped to tell you.' While he was still speaking, another came and said, 'The fire of God fell from heaven and burned up the sheep and the servants, and consumed them; I alone have escaped to tell you'" (1:13-16). A third messenger tells of the robbery of the camels, a fourth the death of the sons and daughters due to a violent wind that battered the house where they were eating and drinking (1:17-20).

This trial, which was certainly a terrible one, elicits a response from Job that is described thus: "Then Job arose, tore his robe, shaved his head, and fell on the ground and worshiped. He said, 'Naked I came from my mother's womb, and naked shall I return there; the Lord gave, and the Lord has taken away; blessed be the name of the Lord.' In all this Job did not sin or charge God with wrong-doing" (1:20-22).

Satan then asks for a second chance to test Job, and he strikes him with a malignant disease "from the sole of his foot to the crown of his head" (2:7). Stripped now not only of all his possessions but even of his physical integrity, Job is looked upon as one cursed by God. Driven from his home, he sits amid the ashes, to indicate that his life now is entirely wretched. "Then his wife said to him, 'Do you still persist in your integrity? Curse God, and die' " (2:9). The wife's literal words are "Bless God and die," but her meaning is clear: Job ought to curse God; the writer uses a less offensive phrase. "But he said to her, 'You speak as any foolish woman would speak. Shall we receive the good at the hands of God, and not receive the bad?' In all this Job did not sin with his lips" (2:10).

The story ends with the news that three friends have come to sympathize with Job and console him. They gaze at him from a distance but do not recognize him; they cry aloud and begin to weep. Then they sit beside him in silence for seven days and seven nights.

Thus far the Prologue.

Some Questions

1. What do the characters stand for?

Job is certainly not a real individual but a kind of laboratory model. He symbolizes human beings who are just and therefore blessed by God; those who do nothing to draw down evil upon them, either through their own actions or through the actions of their children, for Job is accustomed to offer sacrifice every time his children have feasted together, in order to make reparation for any sins they may have committed.

He is not a real individual, because in fact every one of us human beings has sins to repent of and must endure their evil consequences. Job is therefore a fictitious abstract figure that enables us to comprehend one way of knowing God.

It is also worth noting that Job is described with traits that do not link him to any particular religious or confessional tradition. Throughout the book, in fact, the terms characteristic of the Hebrew tradition—covenant, law, temple, Jerusalem, priesthood—are missing. He can be seen as symbolizing any honest human being of good will who has a sense of God and of the mystery of God.

Satan stands for everything that in any way tempts and tests human beings through trials.

2. If these, then, are the two characters that play a part in this opening scene, we may ask ourselves what is the focal point of this very singular drama.

• We may begin by reading once again the question of Satan that gets the whole action started. The Lord says to him: ''Have you considered my servant Job? There is no one like him on earth, a blameless and upright man who fears God and turns away from evil.'' Satan replies: ''Does Job fear God for nothing? Have you not put a fence around him and his house and all that he has, on every side? You have blessed the work of his hands, and his possessions have increased in the land. But stretch out your hand now, and touch all that he has, and he will curse you to your face'' (1:8-11).

The issue here takes the form of a derisive challenge or a wager laid on a human being: Is any human action completely selfless? Is there in fact any exercise of freedom that is untainted and not motivated by some calculation, however subtle? Is it not perhaps the case that everything which goes on in human beings, even in their innermost attitudes, is the result of a calculation, an expectation of profit, a hope of receiving, an ''I'll give to you if you'll give to me in return'' (*do ut des*)?

This is the accusation which each of us feels to be leveled at us deep within and which depth analysis continually brings to the surface: human beings are unable to love without hope of return, and their every action is motivated by some kind of self-interest or even by resentment or a desire for revenge.

Actions truly transparent and clear do not exist, and even the exercise of religion—the highest form of activity available to human beings—springs from the hope of receiving a reward or depends on a reward already received.

Such is the drama in which we are enveloped, for in every situation in which human freedom is at work we want to know whether our action is true, authentic, and selfless, or whether we are seeking some profit. How often we question our choice of vocation, our constancy, our service! Are these the fruit of love for God or are they based on convenience, calculation, inclination, predisposition? In the end we are left desolate because we realize that the real motives for our actions are often shabby.

Satan, the Accuser, claims therefore that authentic religion does not exist; that human beings are incapable of a fully free love, of living the covenant with God. God offers a covenant to them as to equals. His love is authentic and sincere, and he looks for a response of authentic and sincere love, but such a response is not possible; it is a lie, an illusion. Religion is, consequently, an opium for the people; it is a camouflage for motivations that are economic, social, political, psychological, and cultural. Genuine love of God does not exist; God himself is something human beings have invented to disguise and sublimate their real motives. They are in fact playing a game with themselves.

• At the center of the drama recounted in the Prologue there is, however, not only Satan's wager regarding human beings, but also God's wager: the wager of a God who believes in human authenticity and trusts in it.

This, then, is a universal drama. That is, it covers the entire gamut of situations in which human freedom comes into play, and especially those in which unmerited suffering tests human beings and leads them to express what they truly are.

The readers of the Book of Job feel drawn into the struggle because they immediately realize that their own capacity or lack of capacity for authentic existence is at issue. As a contemporary commentator on the Book of Job has put it:

> The sacred writer's picture of Job is too powerful for readers to be indifferent to it. Those who do not enter into the action with their own interior questions and answers, those who are not stimulated to take a position, will not understand a drama that must remain unfinished, as far as they are concerned, because of their lack of participation. But if they do enter into the action and take a position they will find themselves under the gaze of God and be put to the test by the depiction of an eternal, universal drama embodied in the person of Job (L. Alonso Schökel, *Giobbe* [Borla, 1985], 108).

We ask the Lord that we may be drawn into this drama through our rereading of the Prologue of Job. I urge you to meditate on it and to challenge yourselves.

Teachings

In order to help you, I offer some final reflections on the subject of trials.

1. Trials exist, and everyone, even the best of us, has them. There was no reason in Job why he should be tried, since he was perfect in every respect. We must therefore become aware and realize that trials or temptations are a fundamental fact of life.

2. God is mysterious. He knows full well the worth, or lack of it, of all human beings; he knows it before he tests them, and yet he does test them.

The Lord expresses this same thought when he says to the Israelites: "Remember the long way that the Lord your God has led you these forty years in the wilderness, in order to humble you, testing you to know what was in your heart, whether or not you would keep his commandments" (Deut 8:2). This divine way of behaving is, it seems to me, part of that impenetrable mystery in which God, though knowing the Son, put him to the test in the incarnation. For even the incarnation and life of Jesus were a trial.

3. The attitude we should cultivate in trial is submission: acceptance, and not challenge. This attitude emerges in the Prologue as the conclusion and resolution of the trials to which Job is subject, but its stages are developed for us in the course of the poem. "Naked I came from my mother's womb, and naked shall I return there; the Lord gave, and the Lord has taken away; blessed be the name of the Lord . . . Shall we receive the good at the hands of God, and not receive the bad?" (1:21; 2:10). This mysterious submission, the crown of a human life lived in God's presence, is presented to us from the outset as the attitude that ought to inspire us. This does not mean that we already have it, for in Job himself it will be the fruit of all his suffering. It is nonetheless highlighted from the beginning because it alone is able to throw a ray of light on the tragic experience of human life.

4. When we are tried we also run the risk of reflection. With the help of God's grace, human beings can quickly adopt an attitude of submission. Immediately thereafter, however, comes the time of reflection, which is the worst trial of all. The Book of Job might have ended at the end of the second chapter, after showing that Job stood fast because his love of God was real and genuine. In fact, however, we must wait and see, for the situation of Job is not that of a human being who is content to sigh and accept his lot once and for all. Rather it is the concrete situation of a human being who having once expressed acceptance must embody that acceptance day after day. This fact allows the dramatic development that occupies the remainder of the book.

We ourselves have a similar experience at times: when faced with a difficult decision or a momentous event, we are swept along by the enthusiasm and courage that are given to us in life's hard moments. But a little reflection then opens the door to turmoil of mind, and we experience the difficulty of accepting that to which we gave our assent. This is the real trial.

Job's initial assent is that of one whose instinctive reaction is virtuous. The difficulty is to persevere in this assent for a lifetime and under the pressure of feelings and mental conflict.

The initial acceptance, therefore, though it is often a great grace of God, does not yet fully reveal the person's capacity for selfless love. That acceptance must undergo the long testing of everyday life.

Job's trial does not consist so much in his being deprived of all possessions and covered with sores, as in his having to stand fast day after day amid the discourses of his friends and the torrent of arguments that seek to rob him of his sense of what he truly is. Seen from this angle, the trial begins to unfold within the human mind, and the real and lasting temptation, to which we too are subject and to which we risk succumbing, is to let ourselves go astray amid the awful torment of mind, heart, and imagination.

The Book of Humanity's Poorest

I shall add here a final point which you can keep in mind as you meditate: that the Book of Job is a book about the poorest of humanity. I myself received a great deal of enlightenment on this point from a commentary that was given to me last year (in its Italian edition) by its author, Gustavo Gutiérrez: *On Job. God-Talk and the Suffering of the Innocent* (Maryknoll, N.Y.: Orbis Books, 1987). The book is not a work of exegesis proper, but rather a reflection that sheds light on the human side of the Book of Job, in which Gutierrez hears, as he reads, the cry of the Latin American poor.

All of us suffer because of our own mistakes. There is however a vast majority of the human race that suffers beyond its deserts, beyond what its sins may have merited; these are the wretched, suffering, oppressed people who make up perhaps three quarters of humankind. This immense throng gives rise to the question: Why? What meaning does their suffering have? Is it even possible to speak of a meaning?

It is the merit of books like Job, books that move outside the ordinary patterns of life, to face up to so tragic a question.

We, for our part, want to be faithful to Jesus in his trials, and we know that his trials are those of the messianic people, the suffering, the hungry and impoverished. Let us therefore, in our reflections, try to become their neighbors and to accept our own, often minor, trials, while bearing in mind the very great trials that afflict the majority of the human race.

THREE

The Testing of the Rich Young Man

(Homily for Monday of the Twentieth Week of Ordinary Time)
(Readings: Judges 2:11-19; Matthew 19:16-22)

Here in this chapel we have before us a picture of the Madonna which represents her at the moment of the worst trial of her life, the moment of her greatest and most painful temptation. It is a picture of Our Lady of Sorrows.

It reminds us also of Mary's tears, that is, her sharing in our trials as well as in the trials and sufferings of her Son.

"Mary, our Mother, we offer you our days, our lives, and all our efforts to enter more deeply into the mystery of Jesus and share more closely in his trials and his way."

The first reading (Judg 2:11-19) raises a question: What meaning can an Old Testament book have for us that speaks of wars, battles, and slaughters and is certainly remote from our way of experiencing the mystery of God?

On the other hand, we can indeed understand that this book was intended to answer a question which Jews asked themselves as they thought back over the beginnings of their history: How is it that God promised us a land flowing with milk and honey, but then did not give it to us without effort on our part but only as a land that had to be conquered laboriously and at the cost of so much apprehension and suffering?

How is it that he gave it to us for good only after centuries of insecurity and a long period when we were threatened by other peoples and felt like strangers in the land?

Various answers are given to this question, which is really about trials and testings and is the same question that Job asks: Why has God acted thus and not otherwise with me?

For example, in the chapter following upon the passage we have heard read, it is said that God did not want the Israelites to forget the art of war, an art which their fathers had learned in order that they might make their way into the land. Elsewhere it is said that God did not want the land to become wild; when things go too well, people tend to grow lazy and refuse the effort of cultivating the soil. Or again, a reason given in the sapiential books is that God wanted to allow an opportunity for the conversion of other peoples.

The basic reason given in the Book of Judges is that the Israelites did not deserve the gift of the land but rather distanced themselves from the Lord every time the land was given into their possession.

From all this we can derive an important truth: each of us, and the human race as a whole, readily lose our energy when we run along under full sail, when prayer, health, apostolate, friendships, and activities are all going well. Theoretically it should not be so, since human beings are made for happiness and for the enjoyment of abundant gifts. In fact, however, due to their historical condition as persons wounded by sin, in times of prosperity human beings begin to worship idols; they grow proud and worship themselves, their own powers, and the display of their own potentialities, their own physical, social, and intellectual accomplishments.

The Lord tries the Israelites whenever they attain a minimum of peace and prosperity and therefore become idolaters.

Trials are thus to be seen as a way in which God in his providence keeps us on the alert.

As we reflect on our own experience, we are obliged to admit that we would readily fall asleep were it not the continuous small sufferings, the continuous physical and moral stimuli that compel us to keep in trim for the spiritual combat.

There is a mysterious divine providence at work in the fact that the Israelite people are unable to enjoy the peaceful possession of their land right from the outset. A mysterious process is at work purifying individuals and the people by means of troubles and sorrows.

Even if we do not fully understand the reason for this divine way of doing things, we are called to contemplate it as it shows itself in the pilgrimage of the people of God, so that we may accept it, at least in some measure, in our personal lives.

In the gospel passage (Matt 19:16-22) Jesus puts to the test a young man who regarded himself as a very decent person because he had come into full possession of his own estate and his own resources and had subjected these to the law of reason and the law of God. He considered that he had found his place, and he asked: What do I still lack that I do not have? Here I am, ready to go.

Jesus responds quite simply: "If you wish to be perfect, go, sell your possessions, and give the money to the poor, and you will have treasure in heaven; then come, follow me" (v. 21). The young man then realizes that he is still far from the goal: "When the young man heard this word, he went away grieving, for he had many possessions" (v. 22). Here we have the mystery that lurks in trials and reveals itself when persons think themselves secure, as though they had reached the culmination of a spiritual journey. The Lord makes a new request which shows them that they still have a great deal to do. Happy are they who do not find it a stumbling stone.

The young man's tragedy was his failure to realize that this was a trial, a test; he took the Lord's invitation too seriously, so to speak. If he had answered: "You are asking something difficult of me, Lord, and only now are my eyes opened. I do not know if I am able to accept what you propose, but help me; give me your grace.'' If he had had this flash of understanding, his story would have turned out differently.

He did not see that the test given him revealed a weakness which should not have surprised him, for it was a step that would allow him to advance more quickly toward Jesus. As a result, he was saddened and went away.

The young man's situation is one of many in which a trial that is refused leads to a turning in on the self and to death.

"Lord, we are here in your presence to tell you that we are weak; even though we cannot now imagine a demand upon us that would beget a crisis, we know that it exists. Nor shall we be surprised if we have trouble accepting the demand, if we feel it to be repugnant. Rather we shall pray to you: Have pity on us! Show us mercy!

"Mary, Mother of Jesus crucified, set our hearts free with the love and humility that the Lord looked for from the rich young man. Grant that when we find ourselves unable to act or refusing to act, we may make this experience a stepping stone to growth in self-knowledge and in love of your Son. And through the gift of Jesus' death and resurrection, heal our hearts of all their deficiencies, anxieties, and fears, so that they be enlightened by the joy of the divine presence.''

FOUR

Job Cannot Accept Himself

Introduction

I would like, by way of introduction, to mention a difficulty that may prevent us from deriving the greatest possible fruit from our retreat. The difficulty consists in the content of the Book of Job. For this very reason I hesitated for a long time to take it as the text on which to base my reflections.

Even my own grasp of the message came only through a lengthy wrestling with the text, for this is not just a book that talks of human trials. No, the book is itself a trial by reason of the bewildering statements it makes that are not to be found elsewhere in the scriptures.

What means have we of getting over this difficulty?

a) The first means is to wrestle with God as Job does; that is, not to let ourselves be frightened but to tackle the reading of the text and its structure, which is actually rather simple. The problem is to grasp what is being said, and the order and manner in which it is said: Is the book just jumbled poetry or does it argue a thesis?

The fact that this question has not as yet received a definitive answer dictates that we should try to gather the message conveyed on each page. Lord, what are you saying to me? How is what I read a hint as to the way I should speak of you or be silent about you in our world with its tragedies? What has this book to do, Lord, with your mystery and my own, with the mystery of the Church, of human suffering, of the poor?

In recent times it has been repeatedly said, in the controversy with the Jewish world over the Carmel of Auschwitz, that after the Holocaust, it is no longer possible to speak about God; that we can only be silent. The statement has been an arrow in the flesh of some theologians, especially the Germans but also anyone aware of the history of Europe in our century. The question therefore arises: Are we really reduced to silence by certain tragedies? Can we still talk of God as long as the tragedy of Lebanon lasts or the tragedy of hunger in the poor countries?

The Book of Job deals with the sores of humanity, and for this reason we perhaps avoid it since it raises difficulties in talking about God and since we reject a God-talk that upsets our usual categories for dealing with the divine.

This, then, is a book that requires us to wrestle with it in prayer, adoration, questioning, and pleading. This is the first way in which we can help ourselves.

b) The second way, which I have already suggested, is to turn the subject matter of our meditation into personal affective prayer; to let ourselves be drawn into and to pray out of our own experience and the experience of those we love and especially those we see suffering; to pray out of the sufferings of the Church and the human race.

In other words: we must rediscover the psalms of lamentation. When all is said and done, the Book of Job may be regarded as an introduction to this half of the Psalter, a half which we recite but have trouble identifying with: namely, the psalms of lamentation.

I suggest, for example, that as a help in turning today's passage of Job into prayer, you make use of Psalm 88, which has the title (in *The New Jerusalem Bible*) "Prayer in great distress." This is the most pessimistic of all the psalms, for while many other psalms of lamentation end with words expressing requests granted or thanksgiving, the final verse of Psalm 88 is:

"You have deprived me of friends and companions; and all I know is the dark" (v. 18 *NJB*). In what sense, then, is this psalm a prayer? How can I pray it? The challenge posed by the Book of Job is precisely to understand how a situation of great pain and anguish can be lived in faith.

c) It is important, finally, not to let our minds become undisciplined. Each of us must, in light of our adult experience of prayer, set aside periods during the day for silent mental prayer, for reading, and for vocal prayer, which is very useful (especially the rosary). A rhythm of prayer that is adapted to the present phase of our search for God will be extremely useful in overcoming the difficulties raised by the subject matter of the biblical text.

Job Curses the Day of His Birth

Let us reflect on Chapter 3 of Job, asking ourselves first, during the *lectio* or reading, what the text says, and then, during the *meditatio* or meditation, what message the text has for us.

After the seven days and nights during which Job's friends sit beside him on the ground in silence, "Job arose, tore his robe, shaved his head, and fell on the ground and worshiped" (3:1). The content of Chapter 3 is precisely this: a curse on the day of his birth. Job spoke as follows:

> Let the day perish in which I was born,
>> and the night that said,
>> "A man-child is conceived."
> Let that day be darkness!
>> May God above not seek it,
>> or light shine on it.
> Let gloom and deep darkness claim it.
>> Let clouds settle upon it;
>> let the blackness of the day terrify it.
> That night—let thick darkness seize it!
>> let it not rejoice among the days of the year;
>> let it not come into the number of the months.

Yes, let that night be barren;
    let no joyful cry be heard in it.
Let those curse it who curse the Sea,
    those who are skilled to rouse up Leviathan.
Let the stars of its dawn be dark;
    let it hope for light, but have none;
    may it not see the eyelids of the morning—
because it did not shut the doors of my mother's womb,
    and hide trouble from my eyes.
Why did I not die at birth,
    come forth from the womb and expire?
Why were there knees to receive me,
    or breasts for me to suck?
Now I would be lying down and quiet;
    I would be asleep; then I would be at rest
with kings and counselors of the earth
    who rebuild ruins for themselves,
or with princes who have gold,
    who fill their houses with silver.
Or why was I not buried like a stillborn child,
    like an infant that never sees the light?
There the wicked cease from troubling,
    and there the weary are at rest.
There the prisoners are at ease together;
    they do not hear the voice of the taskmaster.
The small and the great are there,
    and the slaves are free from their masters.
Why is light given to one in misery,
    and life to the bitter in soul,
who long for death, but it does not come,
    and dig for it more than for hidden treasures;
who rejoice exceedingly,
    and are glad when they find the grave?
Why is light given to one who cannot see the way,
    whom God has fenced in?
For my sighing comes like my bread,
    and my groanings are poured out like water.
Truly the thing that I fear comes upon me,
    and what I dread befalls me.

> I am not at ease, nor am I quiet;
> I have no rest; but trouble comes (chapter 3).

I have already noted that this chapter rings oddly. The preceding chapter says that Job did not curse God but put up with all the harsh events; now we find that the testing has hardly begun. The act of submission has to find its way into the mind, the heart, and the body of the person who has made it, and this is very difficult.

After seven days of silence, the volcano that has been smoldering in Job's soul now erupts.

I shall divide the text into its four sections.

1. *Vv. 1-10*: the theme here is the curse uttered against the day of his birth. The hour does not matter: "Let that day be darkness! . . . Yes, let that night be barren; let no joyful cry be heard in it" (vv. 4, 7). Job wants to remove that day and night from the course of time, to thrust it back into the primal murk of nonbeing.

This is a theme not often found in the scriptures, which for the most part are a hymn to life. There are, however, some well-known pages that offer a parallel to the loathing Job feels. In the Book of Jeremiah, for example, the prophet exclaims:

> Cursed be the day
>   on which I was born!
> The day when my mother bore me,
>   let it not be blessed!
> Cursed be the man
>   who brought the news to my father, saying,
> "A child is born to you, a son,"
>   making him very glad.
> Let that man be like the cities
>   that the Lord overthrew without pity;
> let him hear a cry in the morning
>   and an alarm at noon,
> because he did not kill me in the womb;
>   so my mother would have been my grave,
>   and her womb forever great.

Why did I come forth from the womb
  to see toil and sorrow,
  and spend my days in shame? (Jer 20:14-18).

I urge you, however, to begin your reading of this chapter of Jeremiah with v. 7.

Jeremiah is a famous and extraordinary person, endowed with an ability to see God's world that is almost unparalleled in history, an ability reserved to very few. And yet he reaches the point where he laments like Job. Job, then, is not utterly singular but gives voice to the most tragic moments of human experience.

2. *Vv. 10-19*: the theme is now not simply Job's abhorrence of his birth, but his longing for death: "Why did I not die at birth, come forth from the womb and expire?" (v. 11).

We may think here of Jonah, who is so dissatisfied with God's action that he becomes depressed and asks the Lord to take his life away: "But this was very displeasing to Jonah, and he became angry. He prayed to the Lord and said, 'O Lord! Is not this what I said while I was still in my own country? That is why I fled to Tarshish at the beginning; for I knew that you are a gracious God and merciful, slow to anger, and abounding in steadfast love, and ready to relent from punishing. And now, O Lord, please take my life from me, for it is better for me to die than to live' " (Jonah 4:1-3).

At the very moment when God's mercy is revealed, the prophet feels undone, he feels that his kind of prophesying has been disavowed; so intense is his irritation, vexation, and rage that he wants to die.

I am reminded here of another extraordinary personage, Elijah. Because he has been unable to overcome the false prophets in the name of Yahweh, he takes flight; frightened by the threats of Queen Jezabel, "he got up and fled for his life, and came to Beersheba, which belongs to Judah; he left his servant there. But he himself went a whole day's journey into the wilderness, and came and sat down under a solitary broom tree. He asked that he might die: 'It is enough; now, Lord, take away my life, for I am no better than my ancestors' '' (1 Kgs 19:3-4).

Although Elijah lived on intimate terms with the mystery of God, he too was deeply vexed by his failure to accomplish what he should have.

3. *Vv. 20-23*: the curse which Job calls down on the day of his birth, and his longing now for death, are generalized, as he expresses life's overall lack of meaning. "Why is light given to one in misery, and life to the bitter in soul, who long for death, but it does not come?'' (vv. 20-21).

4. Finally, in the fourth part of the chapter, *vv. 24-26*, Job returns to his own situation and describes his experience in greater detail:

> For my sighing comes like my bread,
>   and my groanings are poured out like water.
> Truly the thing that I fear comes upon me,
>   and what I dread befalls me.
> I am not at ease, nor am I quiet;
>   I have no rest; but trouble comes (vv. 24-26).

These verses give forceful expression to the cry that breaks the silence of the seven days and nights: Job loathes his birth, desires death, asserts that the lives of all who suffer are without meaning, and, finally, turns back to himself to sum up: Here I am, restless and tormented.

Job's Cry and the Prayer of Lamentation

Let us turn now to meditation on this chapter and ask ourselves: Is Job's language rhetorical? Is it due to the characteristic exaggeration practiced by Orientals, who often use hyperbole? But how, then, can such language find a place in scriptures that have permanent value? Is there anything comparable in our own experience?

I think, for example, of how persons brought up against

the clear prospect of incurable illness not infrequently break out in cries and lamentation. If physicians think it wise to tell patients the stark truth, the first reaction of the latter is always one of emotional rebellion: What is the meaning of it? Why me?

At any moment any one of us can find himself in this situation of extremely serious and incurable illness; then we may well make our own the cry of Job.

Or we might think of people who at some time in their lives pass through a series of hardships and misfortunes that come piling one upon another and lead these individuals to wild anger. The surprising thing is that the Bible does not condemn these sentiments, that it does not exorcise them but keeps them as part of the inspired sacred text.

We may broaden our perspective and ask: What meaning is there for the wretched lives of so many men and women? For a life of extreme penury, deprived of any chance to become properly human? What meaning is there for the throngs of underprivileged folk, of the impoverished, of those who barely subsist and for whom there is no prospect of a way out? When we realize how great is all this misery and how long a time it will take to improve the living conditions of so many people, and when at the same time we run into the political corruption, national and international, that resists the development of peoples, then we cannot help asking ourselves what is the meaning of it all and whether it would not have been better for these afflicted people never to have been born. And what can we say of the children born in underdeveloped countries with their high birth rate, children already sick, handicapped, and hindered in their growth from the very beginning, for lack of necessary care?

Job's cry, then, is one heard in today's world as well, and the radical temptation to long for death threatens everyone without exception. It threatens even those who, though glad that they are not touched by terrible afflictions, cannot turn away from the reality of the downward slope on which so many people are caught.

We are thus led to be more temperate in our judgment of the Bible and more understanding of the legitimacy of Job's cry, which is matched by the way in which the abandoned of every age express their feelings.

It is not an accident that this kind of response has been taken into the scriptures in the form of the prayer of lamentation. In his commentary on the Book of Job, Gustavo Gutiérrez makes this point, following Claus Westermann who maintains that the dominant literary genre in the Book of Job is the lamentation, the declaration of one's wretchedness before God: "Only if this is kept in mind will it be possible to understand correctly the structure of the work [the Book of Job]. At the beginning of his well-known study of Job . . . he [Westermann] writes: 'At the base of my investigation lies the simple recognition that in the Old Testament human suffering has its own peculiar language and that one can understand the structure of the Book of Job only if one has first understood the language of lamentation'" (*On Job* 109, n. 14).

Westermann goes on to point out that contrary to the negative Western view of lamentation as signifying resignation, turning in on oneself, and inability to help oneself, in the Bible it is closely connected with prayer: it is an element in petition, in the invocation of God's help. He also observes that in the young Christian churches this form of prayer is frequently seen to be recovering its rightful place. We need only think, for example, of the intense popular devotion in Latin America to the dead Christ, in which the lamentations also give voice to the sufferings of the poor (see Gutiérrez 111, n. 7).

Toward the end of his book, Gutiérrez cites another contemporary author whose words will help us to understand better the mystery of the prayer of lamentation, a prayer that can at times seem blasphemous:

> The remarkable thing about this Book is that Job makes not a single step of flight to a better God, but stays resolutely in the field of battle under the fire of the divine wrath. Although God treats him as an enemy, through the dark night and the abyss

Job does not falter, nor invoke another court, nor even appeal to the God of his friends, but calls upon this God who crushes him. He flees to the God whom he accuses. He sets his confidence in God who has disillusioned him and reduced him to despair. . . . Without deviating from the violent assertion of his innocence and God's hostility, he confesses his hope, taking as his Defender the One who judges him, as his Liberator the One who throws him in prison, and as his Friend his mortal enemy (R. de Pury, cited in Barth's *Church Dogmatics* and in Gutiérrez 128, n. 1).

A lamentation is a prayer that shakes up the soul, causing the pus to issue from the deepest wounds inflicted on us; it is therefore able also to free us interiorly. For the path followed by Job is one of liberation and purification, enabling him to see the face of God once again and to recover the sense of his own dignity and value.

Suggestions

I suggest four thoughts for your personal and practical meditation on Chapter 3 of Job.

1. We must learn to distinguish lamentation from complaint in our lives. Generally speaking, complaining is much more common because we tend to grumble at everything, while each of us complains of others; it is rare that one does not hear criticism of others in religious, social, and political circles. We have lost the real meaning of lamentation, which means mourning before God. As a result, when the feelings of defiance, irritation, and anger that are aroused in the heart do not find their natural and proper outlet, people let them fly at anyone and anything around them, creating unhappiness in personal life and in families, communities, and groups. Only God, who is our Father, can put up with even the rebellions and cries of his children; it is because our God is so good and strong that we can quarrel with him. He accepts this confrontation, as he

accepted it from Elijah, Jonah, Jeremiah, and Job. It is true that
Jonah was rebuked when he asked to die, but meanwhile God
allowed him to speak.

Releasing the flow of lamentation is the most effective way
of shutting off the streams of complaint that make the world,
society, and the concrete Church such sad places and that are
utterly fruitless because, being utterances simply of human
feeling, they do not get to the bottom of problems.

If we were to substitute profound lamentation in prayer for
barren complaining that only opens new wounds, we would
often find the solution of our problems and those of others or
at least would find a more legitimate way of calling attention
to suffering and hardship in the Church.

I must admit to having been in situations in which, in response to the question: "Where in the Bible can I find something in tune with what I am now feeling?" I found myself
reading the Lamentations of Jeremiah and experiencing peace.
Instead of taking the path of criticism or various forms of revenge and resentment, I allowed the words of the prophet,
intense though they be, to soften and thaw my heart.

The reason why the poor have greater powers of endurance than the rich may be that they have retained this profound, interior outlet, this wisdom about living. Those who
have lost it can respond only with anger; they think they are
masters of the universe, and if things do not go their way they
avenge themselves on others.

2. A second thought. Job does not see the meaning of his
experience and he refuses to accept it.

> My sighing comes like my bread,
>   and my groanings are poured out like water.
> Truly the thing that I fear comes upon me,
>   and what I dread befalls.
> I am not at ease, nor am I quiet;
>   I have no rest; but trouble comes (vv. 24–26).

To use a contemporary term, Job's condition is that of one

who has "lost all motivation," one who can no longer find
any reason to engage in the struggle.

When we find ourselves in this condition, it rings an alarm
bell. When we examine ourselves at moments of uncertainty
and exhaustion and we seem to have lost our motivation, we
feel afraid. And when someone comes to us, perhaps even a
young person only a few years married, and tells us he or she
has lost their motivation, again we are frightened. There are
two reasons for this: first and foremost, we realize that we can
find ourselves in the same condition. Second, the term "loss
of motivation" seems to say that the condition is terminal; it
seems to justify evasions: I no longer feel anything, I no longer
have any desires; what fault is it of mine?

Job tells us, on the contrary, to face up to our condition so
that it will lose something of its malevolent power. He urges
us to look at the condition with courage, to think of it as not
so terrible as to leave us no out. He prods us to ask ourselves
what the condition means, especially since persons who find
themselves lacking motivation have not changed much objec-
tively, except that they are no longer able to understand action which is unselfish.

We saw in the Prologue of Job the wager made by God:
he maintains that human beings are capable of acting out of
unselfish love even when ordinary satisfactions are taken away.
Those who find themselves lacking in motivation should in fact
say to themselves: I have reached the point at which I can, for
the first time in my life, begin to be a human being, because
I no longer have the string of satisfactions which I had before.

Ninety-eight percent of our actions are the result of the ebb
and flow of reciprocal satisfactions that sustain us; and it is
right that it should be so. But the proof that disinterested,
gratuitous love exists comes when we are completely stripped
bare before God and his crucified love. This is the wager taken
in the Book of Job, a man who cries out, and with reason, that
he has lost all motivation, that he desires death, that life no
longer has any meaning, but who cries out before God and

his friends. He continues to stir himself and to act; he continues to seek.

When motivation has been lost, freedom is purified: the freedom about which there could be some doubt, before the wager, as to its capacity for unselfish action. Job the man gradually reaches his true self.

When, therefore, we think we have reached a limit beyond which we cannot advance, we have in fact only reached the point at which our freedom can find its most authentic expression. Jesus manifested the selflessness of his love not only when he performed miracles but also on the cross, for then two selfless loves came face to face and matched each other.

Let us learn from Job that our human dignity shows itself in loving God even when the lack of motivation has reached the extreme that is expressed in the words on which we have reflected.

If we find in ourselves any root of frustration, if we are frightened lest our actions have no meaning, and if we are afraid even to acknowledge this fact, we should try to say as much to God in the form of a lamentation.

3. We must accept ourselves as we are. When we speak of the poor, for example, we are always tormented that we cannot really share their situation. For, since we have in fact received a formation and an education, we will never be like the poor, no matter what may befall us.

How, then, are we to behave? Like the people back in 1968 who forced themselves to wear unkempt beards and go around dirty so that they might in some degree be like those who are deprived of everything?

That would be absurd. We should thank the Lord that we are who we are, and then ask ourselves what we can do, here and now, for the brothers and sisters who are different from us. We should ask ourselves what we can receive from them who in their turn will ask us the same questions. The important thing is that I should respond to God and that I should love others as much as I can. The desire to get out of myself is a form of Mephisthophelean pretension.

Job helps us to tear down these castles in the air, to be able humbly to accept ourselves and to accept our brothers and sisters, because we are in this world to give ourselves to one another. The claim that we can enter into the skins of all so as to have a geometrically perfect solution proves in the end to be sensationally mistaken.

How often, for example, we think we can help the African peoples in their poverty and are completely mistaken, for we make gestures and adopt attitudes that are not accepted.

If, on the other hand, I set about to listen with love to these peoples, I find that I can receive a great deal from them; and even if I do not completely understand their outlook, I experience existential exchanges that allow me to say: Lord, I have done what I can in the following of your Son; now show me your mercy.

Such modesty of judgment, which inevitably requires intellectual sacrifices, is difficult and is acquired only with age and experience. When we are young we do not accept limits on our intellectual capacity to know everything, to know ourselves completely, and to assess others completely, in the light of ourselves.

4. Finally, I would like to remind you of the title of this retreat: "You have stood by me in my trials."

Let us ask Jesus in the Garden of Olives: "Lord, did you ever experience moments in which everything seemed to you to be bizarre, insipid, and meaningless, moments in which you had no desire to do anything and felt no spur of any kind to action? And how did you live through such moments?"

St. Charles Borromeo tells us that he experienced frustration, a sense of uselessness and disgust. One day, when his cousin Frederick asked him how he acted at such moments, he showed him the little Psalter which he always carried in his pocket. He fell back on the songs of lamentation in order to give voice to his own suffering and, at the same time, to recover his staying power and confidence in the presence of the mystery of the living God.

Let us pray that the Lord will give us, too, the gift of being able to approach the purifying and restorative fountain of biblical lamentation.

FIVE

Job's Examination of Conscience

The theological risk which readers of the Book of Job run is nicely brought out, I think, in a passage which I found in an article of philosopher Emanuele Severino, entitled "The Danger to Faith in Socratic Irony." Severino writes:

> When King Midas wanted to know what is best and most desirable for a human being, Silenus [who represented the tradition of Dionysiac wisdom] was silent for a long time and then replied: "Member of a wretched and ephemeral race, child of chance and suffering, why do you force me to tell you what it is most to your advantage not to hear? That which is best is utterly beyond attainment for you: not to be born, not to be, to be nothing. But the second best for you is to die soon" (that is, to return as soon as possible to nothingness) (*Corriere della Sera*, August 21, 1989).

The theological problem posed by Job can be brought out by a question: What is the difference between words of the kind I have just cited and the words we find in Chapter 3 of Job?

The language sounds the same to some extent and the words are at times even identical, and yet the difference between the two writings is enormous, for the man who speaks in the biblical book is neither a sceptic nor someone disappointed by life.

We are asked, then, to enter into the abyss of true and mysterious knowledge of God, of a God who is ineffable.

We fear doing so. It is likely that if the Book of Job were presented today to a doctrinal or theological commission for a decision whether or not to accept it as part of the canon, the decision would be not to admit it lest it cause uneasiness and prove disturbing.

The fact, however, that the book is indeed God's word and part of the canon urges us to take on the labor of reading it. As we read, let us ask the Lord to grant us the spirit of prayer, humility, and adoration, so that we may not let ourselves be ensnared by the purely rational language associated with this knowledge. Limitless mysteries call for a limitless love, and we want to overcome an initial sense of uneasiness and travel the difficult ways of the Word without knowing in advance where he is leading us.

"Lord, give us a true, new, and deeper understanding of you. Grant that even through words which we do not understand the affections of the heart may bring us insight into your mystery which is beyond all understanding.

"Grant that the exercise of intellectual patience and the thorn-strewn journey of the mind may be the sign of a truth which is not attained simply by following the norms of human reason but transcends the universe and, for that reason, is limitless light as well as mystery that is inaccessible but at the same time nourishes the life of human beings by its dramatic turns and its seeming absurdities.

"Grant that we may know you and know ourselves, that we may know the sufferings of humankind and the troubles with which many hearts have to struggle, so that we may have an ever new and truer experience of you."

Job's Final Monologue

Since I cannot possibly read through the entire Book of Job, I shall skip over the intervening chapters and offer some thoughts on Chapters 29, 30, and 31, which contain the magnificent and lengthy final monologue of Job.

Job's monologue in Chapter 3 is followed by three scenes in which each of the three friends address him and he replies. Then comes a mysterious interlude, a kind of lightning flash from on high, namely, the hymn to wisdom (Chapter 28).

Job then launches into a further monologue, the last one before his dialogue with God.

Because these three chapters serve as summary, synthesis, and conclusion, I think it useful to suggest a reading of them in two phases: first, reading proper; then, meditation.

Job's examination of conscience will help us prepare for our own examination of conscience in view of tomorrow, which is a day of reconciliation.

I shall make use primarily of the explanation which Don Gianfranco Ravasi gives of these three chapters in his commentary on Job (*Giobbe* [Borla, 1979]). In his explanation he carefully divides the text into sections that match its internal divisions; in doing so, he offers a first key for reading the chapters.

Chapter 29 is entitled: "Nostalgic song of the past." All the verbs are in the past tense, as Job recalls the situations and surroundings of his life.

Chapter 30 in entitled: "Song of the present and its terrors." It begins with the words "But now . . . ."

Chapter 31 is entitled: "Song of the future and of innocence." As he looks back over his past life, Job makes a very detailed confession or protestation of innocence, starting with a series of ethical norms which he looks at one by one. He ends by relying on God to take his side against God himself.

1.   Chapter 29.

> Job again took up his discourse and said:
> "Oh, that I were as in the months of old,
>   as in the days when God watched over me;
> when his lamp shone over my head,
>   and by his light I walked through darkness;

> when I was in my prime,
>> when the friendship of God was upon my tent;
> when the Almighty was still with me,
>> when my children were around me;
> when my steps were washed with milk,
>> and the rocks poured out for me streams of oil!'' (vv. 1–6).

In this first stanza Job describes himself as one who has experienced the joy of being a friend of God. He felt God's presence when he prayed and in his daily life with its troubles; he tasted God's continuous nearness.

> "When I went out to the gate of the city,
>> when I took my seat in the square,
> the young men saw me and withdrew,
>> and the aged rose up and stood;
> the nobles refrained from talking,
>> and laid their hands on their mouths;
> the voices of princes were hushed,
>> and their tongues stuck to the roof of their mouths.
> When the ear heard, it commended me,
>> and when the eye saw, it approved'' (vv. 7–11).

In this second scene Job describes not only his close relationship with the mystery of God but also his relations with the people of the town.

> ". . . I delivered the poor who cried,
>> and the orphan who had no helper.
> The blessing of the wretched came upon me,
>> and I caused the widow's heart to sing for joy.
> I put on righteousness, and it clothed me;
>> my justice was like a robe and a turban.
> I was eyes to the blind,
>> and feet to the lame.
> I was a father to the needy,
>> and I championed the cause of the stranger.
> I broke the fangs of the unrighteous,
>> and made them drop their prey from their teeth'' (vv. 12–17).

Job was an upright man with an active concern for the poor; those who saw him testified to this. From a defense focused solely on himself, Job has gradually passed to the social aspect; suffering opened his eyes to the need of a concern for the most destitute, the dispossessed.

> "Then I thought, 'I shall die in my nest,
>   and I shall multiply my days like the phoenix;
> my roots spread out to the waters,
>   with the dew all night on my branches;
> my glory was fresh with me,
>   and my bow ever new in my hand' " (vv. 18–20).

Here was his dream for his old age: he was sure that he would continue to bear fruit like one forever young.

> "They listened to me and waited,
>   and kept silence for my counsel.
> After I spoke they did not speak again
>   and my word dropped upon them like dew.
> They waited for me as for the rain;
>   they opened their mouths as for the spring rain.
> I smiled on them when they had no confidence;
>   and the light of my countenance they did not extinguish.
> I chose their way, and sat as chief,
>   and I lived like a king among his troops,
>   like one who comforts mourners" (vv. 21–25).

In this final scene, Job takes a step back into the past, as it were, and recalls his more specifically political involvement, and the power of his presence in society.

Job was upright and good, and he loved the poor. But he was also rewarded, revered, listened to, and esteemed. That entire situation has now been called into question by the new turn his story has taken.

2. Chapter 30. Ravasi divides this "song of the present and its terrors" into seven short sections which describe the successive feelings of a person who descends ever further down

the ladder: humiliated, scorned, attacked, terrified, opposed
by God, weeping, and suffering.

Job humiliated:

> "But now they make sport of me,
>> those who are younger than I,
> whose fathers I would have disdained
>> to set with the dogs of my flock.
> What could I gain from the strength of their hands?
>> All their vigor is gone.
> Through want and hard hunger
>> they gnaw the dry and desolate ground,
> they pick mallow and the leaves of the bushes,
>> and to warm themselves the roots of broom.
> They are driven out from society;
>> people shout after them as after a thief.
> In the gullies of wadis they must live,
>> in holes in the ground, and in the rocks.
> Among the bushes they bray;
>> under the nettles they huddle together.
> A senseless, disreputable brood,
>> they have been whipped out of the land" (vv. 1–8).

Job scorned:

> "And now they mock me in song;
>> I am a byword to them.
> They abhor me, they keep aloof from me;
>> they do not hesitate to spit at the sight of me" (vv. 9–10).

Job attacked:

> "Because God has loosed my bowstring and humbled me,
>> they have cast off restraint in my presence.
> On my right hand the rabble rise up;
>> they send me sprawling,
>> and build roads for my ruin.
> They break up my path,
>> they promote my calamity;
>> no one restrains them.

As through a wide breach they come;
   amid the crash they roll on" (vv. 11-14).

But God is the real, though anonymous, warrior—"he"—
who does battle against a man now humiliated and scorned.
Job terrified:

"Terrors are turned upon me;
   my honor is pursued as by the wind,
   and my prosperity has passed away like a cloud.
And now my soul is poured out within me;
   days of affliction have taken hold of me.
The night racks my bones,
   and the pain that gnaws me takes no rest.
With violence he grasps my garment;
   he grasps me by the collar of my tunic.
He has cast me into the mire,
   and I have become like dust and ashes" (vv. 15-19).

And, as if this were not enough, God opposes him:

"I cry to you and you do not answer me;
   I stand and you merely look at me.
You have turned cruel to me;
   with the might of your hand you persecute me.
You lift me up on the wind, you make me ride on it,
   and you toss me about in the roar of the storm.
I know that you will bring me to death,
   and to the house appointed for all living" (vv. 20-23).

Therefore Job is a man who weeps:

"Surely one does not turn against the needy.
   when in disaster they cry for help.
Did I not weep for those whose day was hard?
   Was not my soul grieved for the poor?
But when I looked for good, evil came;
   and when I waited for light, darkness came.
My inward parts are in turmoil, and are never still;
   days of affliction come to meet me" (vv. 24-27).

Abandoned now, Job lives in deepest darkness and is unhappy and suffering:

> "I go about in sunless gloom;
>   I stand up in the assembly and cry for help.
> I am a brother of jackals,
>   and a companion of ostriches.
> My skin turns black and falls from me,
>   and my bones burn with heat.
> My lyre is turned to mourning,
>   and my pipe to the voice of those who weep" (vv. 28–31).

3. Chapter 31. After describing his own present terrible situation, this man rebounds and launches into a "song of the future and of innocence."

> "I have made a covenant with my eyes;
>   how then could I look upon a virgin?
> What would be my portion from God above,
>   and my heritage from the Almighty on high?
> Does not calamity befall the unrighteous,
>   and disaster the workers of iniquity?
> Does he not see my ways,
>   and number all my steps?
> If I have walked with falsehood,
>   and my foot has hurried to deceit—
> let me be weighed in a just balance,
>   and let God know my integrity!—
> if my step has turned aside from the way,
>   and my heart has followed my eyes,
>   and if any spot has clung to my hands;
> then let me sow, and another eat;
>   and let what grows for me be rooted out.
> If my heart has been enticed by a woman,
>   and I have lain in wait at my neighbor's door;
> then let my wife grind for another
>   and let other men kneel over her.
> For that would be a heinous crime;
>   that would be a criminal offense;
> for that would be a fire consuming down to Abaddon,
>   and it would burn to the root all my harvest" (vv. 1–12).

The tone has now completely changed, and the language is that of a confession or protestation regarding individual and social morality.

Job declares himself innocent of sins of unchastity, lying, and adultery. In this context, Ravasi cites some interesting parallels from Semitic antiquity, at a period when it was thought that the dead who present themselves to the gods protest their innocence. One such is a formulary from the Egyptian *Book of the Dead*:

> I have not committed sins against human beings,
> I have not mistreated cattle.
> I have not blasphemed against God.
> I have not struck the wretched.
> I have not caused diseases.
> I have not starved anyone.
> I have not murdered anyone.
> I have not stolen loaves from the spirits.
> I have not committed pederasty.
> I have not done impure actions.
> I have not falsified measures of produce. . . .

The dead cried out these ritual invocations as they sat in the boat carrying them across the river: if the protestations were true, the individuals were not burned; otherwise they were consumed by fire.

But Job's words are not strictly concerned with ritual and judgment; rather, as I said above, they are concerned with morality.

Job then protests his innocence in regard to his slaves, whom he has always treated justly:

> "If I have rejected the cause of my male or female slaves,
>   when they brought a complaint against me;
> what then shall I do when God rises up?
>   When he makes inquiry, what shall I answer him?
> Did not he who made me in the womb make them:
>   And did not one fashion us in the womb?" (vv. 13–15).

Job then defends himself against the charge made by
Eliphaz and declares that he has been charitable to the poor:

"If I have withheld anything that the poor desired,
    or have caused the eyes of the widow to fail,
or have eaten my morsel alone,
    and the orphan has not eaten from it—
for from my youth I have reared the orphan like a father,
    and from my mother's womb I have guided the widow—
if I have seen anyone perish for lack of clothing,
    or a poor person without covering,
whose loins have not blessed me,
    and who was not warmed with the fleece of my sheep;
if I have raised my hand against the orphan,
    because I saw I had supporters at the gate;
then let my shoulder blade fall from my shoulder,
    and let my arm be broken from its socket.
For I was in terror of calamity from God,
    and I could not have faced his majesty" (vv. 16–23).

As for the charge that he has misused his wealth and has
been an idolater, Job declares:

"If I have made gold my trust,
    or called fine gold my confidence;
if I have rejoiced because my wealth was great,
    or because my hand had gotten much;
if I have looked at the sun when it shone,
    or the moon moving in splendor,
and my heart has been secretly enticed,
    and my mouth has kissed my hand;
this also would be an iniquity to be punished by judges,
    for I should have been false to God above" (vv. 24–28).

Job also defends himself against the accusation of hatred
and of having violated hospitality:

"If I have rejoiced at the ruin of those who hate me,
    or exulted when evil overtook them—
I have not let my mouth sin
    by asking for their lives with a curse—

if those of my tent ever said,
  'O that we might be sated with his flesh!'—
the stranger has not lodged in the street;
  I have opened my doors to the traveler—" (vv. 29–32).

Finally, he responds to the charge of hypocrisy and exploitation:

"I have not concealed my transgressions as others do,
  by hiding my iniquity in my bosom,
because I stood in great fear of the multitude,
  and the contempt of families terrified me,
  so that I kept silence, and did not go out of doors. . . .
If my land has cried out against me,
  and its furrows have wept together;
if I have eaten its yield without payment,
  and caused the death of its owners;
let thorns grow instead of wheat,
  and foul weeds instead of barley" (vv. 33–34, 38–40).

Here, then, is Job's lengthy examination of social conscience; he finds himself upright in all the various phases of human life.

Vv. 35–37 are as it were a final challenge to God. For if God is just he cannot remain silent but must endorse Job's confession:

"Oh, that I had one to hear me!
  (Here is my signature! let the Almighty answer me!)
  Oh, that I had the indictment written by my adversary!
Surely I would carry it on my shoulder;
  I would bind it on me like a crown;
I would give him an account of all my steps;
  like a prince I would approach him" (vv. 35–37).

So ends this very lengthy and wide-ranging monologue of Job, a discourse rich in poetry and full of images. We ought to reread it attentively and try to enter into the mystery of the human person and the mystery of God, which find expression here.

Start for the Meditation

I suggest three thoughts that can help in personal meditation and inquiry.

The first is that such a person as Job never existed. He is clearly the projection of a theory, a limit case, an example of a paradisal Adam who always does only what is good.

Why, then, should we try to understand this hypothetical human being who summons the entire world to judgment as he proclaims that he has never harmed anyone or had even a moment of failure?

We try to understand him in order to persuade ourselves that even if a man like Job existed, even he would not be exempt from the tragic trial described in Chapter 30.

Trials are therefore inherent in the relationship between God and human beings, for since this relationship is based on selfless love and not simply on commutative justice, it includes trials.

But one who could truthfully ask "Which of you will convict me of sin?" did exist, and his name is Jesus. He was not exempt from the testing of his selfless love for us. This means that trials are not linked exclusively with sin, purification, and the overcoming of situations of unauthenticity. They are connected rather with the reality of free relationships between human beings and God, with the unqualified gratuitousness which is proper to these relationships and which emerges at the moment when gratifications cease.

The author of the Book of Job is looking for an aspect of the mystery of God that will give trials a meaning beyond that of purification from sin.

This aspect we see in the crucified Jesus.

Our condition, however, is quite different from that of Job the just man, and we can retrace our steps through Chapter 29 and then Chapter 31, asking ourselves: Where do we stand in regard to the circumstances and relationships of our lives, in regard to our ethical obligations? What are our sins of commission and of omission?

We ought to accuse ourselves of these sins not simply in order to avoid punishment and to restore a relationship with God that is based on justice, but in order to strive for that perfect sorrow that springs from love, thus putting into practice what the experience of Job teaches us in its mysterious way. We ought to admit our sins out of pure love, in order that God may be blessed, praised, and sanctified and in order that we may enter into a covenant relationship with him.

We are called to the freedom of an authentic relationship with God, to be constant in living our life as his friends: "I do not call you servants, but friends. You are those who have stood by me in my trials, out of love for me and not simply to be faithful to yourselves and your resolutions."

The pages that recount the drama of Job gives us a glimpse of this radical search of the human heart in its longing for a relationship with God that goes beyond mere obedience and mere justice, a relationship that brings into play the freedom each of us has to give ourselves, to bestow ourselves, to dedicate ourselves selflessly and wholeheartedly.

"Grant, Lord, that as we follow the difficult course set for us in this book of the Bible, we may understand your longing to make us like yourself, your longing to make us like your Son and to bring us into a trinitarian relationship, into that mystery of love and self-giving that is your very essence. Mary, Mother of Jesus and our Mother, grant that we too may enjoy some spark of the innermost mystery of God."

SIX

Blessed among Women

(Homily for the Memorial of Mary the Queen)
(Readings: Isaiah 9:2-4, 6-7; Luke 1:39-47)

The Memorial of the Blessed Virgin Mary, Queen, which is celebrated on the octave of the Assumption, falls auspiciously on the second day of our retreat, for it reminds us that we should be spending these days in union with Mary and imitating her in his listening to the word and in her affective prayer.

We are not asked to acquire new insights, though these are, of course, useful. We are asked rather to expand our hearts by affective prayer and by remaining close to Jesus, as Mary did for long periods, often of silence, and to feed our spirits with the interior affectivity that is so important for perseverance on the spiritual journey.

We may think of today's gospel (Luke 1:39-47) as marking the beginning of the blessings bestowed on Mary, as the first proclamation of her beatitudes: "Blessed are you among women, and blessed is the fruit of your womb. . . . Blessed is she who believed that there would be a fulfillment of what was spoken to her by the Lord."

These words seem like a response to the exclamation of Jeremiah: "Cursed be the day on which I was born!" (Jer 20:14). For here God's work in Mary is exalted, and the exaltation finds expression in jubilation. In human beings the intensity of this jubilation depends on how profound a sense they have of the solitude and despair to which they can fall prey apart from the mystery of God. As the prophet Isaiah says, the increase of joy and gladness—joy such as the harvest brings, exultation such as accompanies the division of spoils—seems proportioned to the darkness in which the people hitherto walked when they "lived in a land of deep darkness" (see Isa 9:2-4).

It is, then, the awareness of darkness and of the meaninglessness to which each of us is condemned by humanity's sinful condition, that makes the mystery of God's love shine out all the more brightly and brings us all the more joy and exultation.

In Mary can be seen the blessedness of every woman and every man who feels enveloped in the mystery of God's covenant: "Blessed are you among women, blessed is the fruit of your womb, blessed is she who believed."

If, however, we consider what Mary's real lot was, we realize that after the proclamation of these words which speak of her as bathed in a river of light, she entered once more into darkness. The events of her life which she did not understand outnumbered those in which she could see the prophecy fulfilled: the birth of her son in poverty, his desertion by so many, his life in which nothing of the greatness foretold by the angel was to be seen.

For years on end Mary experienced a profound grief, for though she enjoyed his direct presence she also knew that he was surrounded by a world utterly ignorant of him.

The Virgin accepted this very hard trial; she continued her pilgrimage of faith to the moment of darkness on Calvary. The blessing spoken upon her at the beginning did not do away with any of the successive trials of her life; it was simply a statement that remained with her in her faith and her trust in God.

In this Eucharist, then, let us entrust to our Lady all of our own darknesses and the darknesses that mark the journey of those we know, those who are dear to us, those who are close to us, and for whom we pray. These are the darknesses in which the great majority of men and women in this world walk. And let us ask the Lord to make us understand that we have all been blessed in Jesus, and that the joy which flooded the hearts of Mary and Elizabeth will also be ours when we glimpse, even from a distance, the mysterious riches contained in the words of the Lord.

"Mary, help us to enter into the mystery of your testing so that we too may henceforth say: 'My soul magnifies the Lord.'

"Grant that even from the valley of our darkness we may be able to cry: 'My spirit rejoices in God my Savior.'

"Teach us to ask ourselves whether this is indeed our daily outlook, whether we are capable of arising from lamentation to glorification of the mystery of God and of abandoning ourselves to the mystery which irrevocably holds us in its arms, be we in darkness or in light.

"Grant that like you we may understand the mystery of the covenant and entrust ourselves to it."

SEVEN

Moderation and Knowledge

"Lord, our God, you are inaccessible mystery; you dwell in an eternal light which no one can look upon except your Son, who revealed it to us from aloft on the cross. Grant that we may enter into the mystery of Jesus so as to understand something of you by the grace of the Holy Spirit. Grant that we may enter into this mystery patiently, humbly, and with a conviction of our ignorance and all that we do not yet understand about your Trinity of love and your plan of salvation. Teach us to be humble in our ignorance, so that we may merit at least some tiny crumb of knowledge of this mystery which will satisfy our hunger forever. We ask this of you through the intercession of Mary whose faith was profound though she had no direct knowledge, and who has gone before us, and even in our name, to the unmediated knowledge of your glory."

We have listened to Job; let us listen now to his partner, God. This will be a way of advancing toward true knowledge of his mystery. In order to divide the way into stages, I have decided to offer reflections on three different chapters of the Book of Job.

First, there is Chapter 9, in which Job speaks about God; then, Chapter 28, in which some anonymous person speaks of God; and, finally, Chapters 38 and 39, in which God himself begins to speak.

Job Refuses to Accept Self-ignorance

Chapter 9 contains Job's response to words which his third friend, Bildad the Shuhite, intends as comforting. Bildad had emphasized the point that there can never be any doubt about the justice of God; and since he is just, the wicked are punished and the good are rewarded. Job, then, can be confident, for his enemies will be covered with shame (see 8:20-22). Job immediately answers by accepting the fundamental principle, and even making things harder for himself: "Indeed I know that this is so; but how can a mortal be just before God?" (9:2).

In the verses that follow, Job expresses this absolute certainty in a somewhat ironic manner: no one can hold out against God, who is always right in every respect and in every instance. Then he adds: "How then can I answer him, choosing my words with him?" (v. 14). Here his self-assurance changes into deeply-felt doubt: God is so right that even if I too were right, I could not win recognition of this fact. From this verse on, therefore, Job begins to have doubts about himself: Who, then, am I? Am I right or wrong?

His words are typical of the outlook of persons who find themselves in the depths of suffering. This outlook might be described as follows: Job refuses to accept self-ignorance; he is goaded and tormented by his inability to know with certainty whether or not he is just; he is convinced that he is indeed an upright man, but he would like this to be told him; uncertainty gnaws at him.

> Though I am innocent, I cannot answer him;
>   I must appeal for mercy to my accuser.
> If I summoned him and he answered me,
>   I do not believe that he would listen to my voice.
> For he crushes me with a tempest,
>   and multiplies my wounds without causes;
> he will not let me get my breath,
>   but fills me with bitterness.
> If it is a contest of strength, he is the strong one!
>   If it is a matter of justice, who can summon him?

> Though I am innocent, my own mouth would condemn me;
> though I am blameless, he would prove me perverse
> (vv. 15–20).

In verse 21 Job makes a dramatic statement and continues on from there:

> I am blameless; I do not know myself;
>   I loathe my life.
> It is all one; therefore I say,
>   he destroys both the blameless and the wicked.
> When disaster brings sudden death,
>   he mocks at the calamity of the innocent.
> The earth is given into the hand of the wicked;
>   he covers the eyes of its judges—
> if it is not he, then who is it? (vv. 21–24).

Job has reached the climax of suffering: he no longer understands anything, he no longer knows who he is. He thinks he is a just man, but he does not know what difference there is between the just and the unjust, nor can he justify himself. In other words, he is losing his own sense of identity: If only I knew why I am in this state!

I have dwelt on this theme because, even though in the Book of Job it finds expression in an extreme and paradoxical case, it applies to a rather common situation, for many individuals suffer agonies about their identity, even if in a degree that is not always tragic. In particular, this affliction besets all those who have responsibilities that do not follow a strict program. Employees of a bank, for example, may find the work burdensome, but they know what their duties are and that their careers depend on how they carry out these duties. Parents, however, have responsibilities that are not defined with geometric precision, and they torture themselves with the question: "What does being a parent mean today? To what extent does this state commit me, oblige me, involve me?" The same holds for educators and pastors, especially when things do not go entirely well and when they do not receive the approval they expect; then they say to themselves: "If only I knew whether I am doing well or poorly; if only I knew what I ought to do; if only I knew whether I am doing all that I ought to do." Uncertainty about their role torments them: "What are my exact responsibilities? What is expected of me, and what can I do to win praise?"

Job thus also represents this painful uncertainty about ourselves, as well as the desire to know that we are radically judged and to be justified fully and clearly in regard to what we do and what pertains to us.

Wisdom Is Beyond All Understanding

Job, then, will not accept the lack of thorough self-knowledge. In the light of this refusal, let us read some passages from the mysterious Chapter 28, the presence of which no one has been able to explain. No speaker is identified here as in the preceding dialogues; suddenly we have a discourse, which some scholars call an "intermezzo." The *New Jerusalem Bible* notes that "the original position and significance of this poem in the Dialogue are far from clear" (p. 787). Nor can we even explain why the passage is included; yet, despite this obscurity, it brings us close to the heart of our subject.

The chapter is concretely a eulogy, a glorification of divine wisdom. The emphasis, however, is on the fact that human beings do not know this wisdom. The chapter begins thus:

> Surely there is a mine for silver,
>   and a place for gold to be refined.
> Iron is taken out of the earth,
>   and copper is smelted from ore.
> Miners put an end to darkness,
>   and search out to the farthest bound
>   the ore in gloom and deep darkness. . . .
> As for the earth, out of it comes bread;
>   but underneath it is turned up as by fire.
> Its stones are the place of sapphires,
>   and its dust contains gold.

That path no bird of prey knows,
    and the falcon's eye has not seen it.
The proud wild animals have not trodden it;
    the lion has not passed over it (vv. 1–8).

The discourse goes on to say, by means of very beautiful poetic images, that everything is attainable except wisdom:

But where shall wisdom be found?
    And where is the place of understanding? (v. 12).

Then begin the "nots":

Mortals do not know the way to it,
    and it is not found in the land of the living.
The deep says, "It is not in me,"
    and the sea says, "It is not in me."
It cannot be gotten for gold,
    and silver cannot be weighed out as its price.
It cannot be valued in the gold of Ophir,
    in precious onyx or sapphire.
Gold and glass cannot equal it,
    nor can it be exchanged for jewels of fine gold. . . .
        (vv. 13–19).

It is worth noting how emphatically the claim is made that wisdom is not to be found or bought or sold. This fact makes the speaker repeat his earlier question: "Where then does wisdom come from? And where is the place of understanding?" (v. 20).

His answer is unchanged:

It is hidden from the eyes of all living,
    and concealed from the birds of the air.
Abaddon and Death say:
    "We have heard a rumor of it with our ears" (vv. 21–22).

Finally, the key to the entire chapter is stated:

God [alone] understands the way to it,
    and he [alone] knows its place . . . (vv. 23ff.)

and the conclusion to be drawn:

> Truly, the fear of the Lord, that is wisdom,
> and to depart from evil is understanding (v. 28).

I regard as especially beautiful the repeated use of "alone" with the references to God, for this word (alone; only) represents a decisive moment in the Bible's understanding of the living God. We find the same word used at times in the Psalms in their effort to proclaim the transcendence of God and, at the same time, his self-communication: He "alone does great wonders," he alone created the heavens; "I will both lie down and sleep in peace; for you alone, O Lord, make me lie down in safety" (Ps 136:4; 4:8).

In the Bible, profound insight into the oneness of God is always accompanied by the assertion that in him alone is our rest, our salvation, our peace.

In Chapter 28, then, we catch sight of an important step forward: human beings do not know themselves nor should they claim to know themselves; rather, let them entrust to God, and to him alone, their uprightness, their self-knowledge, the certainty about their truth to themselves and about their existence.

The chapter is, then, a quiet response to the anxiety experienced by Job, who desires to possess and know himself and wants the security, in heaven and on earth, of being a just man, a man whose life is in order.

God's Answer

We may now turn to the addresses of God, who after being invoked at the beginning of the book and then called to judgment and abused and insulted, has always listened calmly and without getting upset. We may think that he has even listened with love, good will, and kindness to the ravings of Job and his friends.

I shall reflect on some verses of Chapters 38 and 39, and

leave it to you to read and meditate on these chapters in their entirety.

"Then the Lord answered Job out of the whirlwind" (38:1). This theophany recalls the incident in which Elijah the prophet finally grasped something of an ineffable mystery.

God answers by raining down on Job a flood of questions. Job has continually asked questions of God, and God now replies by questioning him.

> Who is this that darkens counsel
>   by words without knowledge?
> Gird up your loins like a man,
>   I will question you, and you shall declare to me.

(Note the ironic tone: "See, I make myself your pupil!")

> Where were you when I laid the foundations of the earth?
>   Tell me, if you have understanding.
> Who determined its measurements—surely you know!
>   Or who stretched the line upon it?
> On what were its bases sunk,
>   or who laid its cornerstone
> when the morning stars sang together
>   and all the heavenly beings shouted for joy? (vv. 4–7).

The question "Where were you?"—the kind of question that evokes deep feeling in those who hear it—turns into a different kind of question: How did this thing come about, and how did that other take place?

Further on, other questions:

> Have you entered into the springs of the sea,
>   or walked in the recesses of the deep?
> Have the gates of death been revealed to you,
>   or have you seen the gates of deep darkness?
> Have you comprehended the expanse of the earth?
>   Declare, if you know all this (vv. 16–18).

The series of questions continues for the remainder of this chapter and the first two verses of Chapter 39. God then turns to a description of the reality which human beings see around them in the animal world, but which they cannot explain fully.

Start for the Meditation

There are numerous lines along which we might reflect in our meditation. One, for example, would be to consider the possibility, or lack of it, that nature may reveal the mystery of God to us, and therefore the possibility that nature may supply a basis for speaking about God. This is a constant preoccupation of contemporary theology, especially in connection with the major themes of ecology: How are we to conceive the presence of God in creation?

I shall not follow that line of thought, however, but shall continue with some reflections on the theme of Job's refusal to accept limits on his knowledge. This seems to me to be a rather important element in the teaching provided by the Book of Job.

1. First consideration: I must accept that I cannot comprehend the universe, that I cannot fully comprehend the plans of God and the Church, or even the full range of my own responsibilities.

This may be hard to accept, since our age is rightly proud of its scientific progress and since even the human sciences aspire, at least unconsciously, to grasp the totality of the mystery.

It seems to me, however, that authentic wisdom requires the recognition that we do not and cannot know everything; that any and every science by its nature deals with a single sector of reality and understands only one aspect of reality.

This limitation on our knowledge torments and humiliates us once we experience the constant temptation of trying to possess the whole of reality so that we may be able to foresee the future. In the final analysis, this temptation goes back to the original human temptation: I want to eat from the tree of the knowledge of good and evil; I want the key to the totality of being, to the totality of God's mysterious plan and of the Church and of the future of our society. Authentic wisdom, on the other hand, springs from acceptance of our human limitations.

2. Second consideration: I must therefore accept that I do not know myself completely. As St. Paul says, even though I am not conscious of having harmed anyone, I am not therefore justified; it is the Lord who justifies me (see 1 Cor 4:3-4).

God alone has total knowledge, which includes knowledge of my life. This is the next step in wisdom, one so difficult for Job and human beings generally to understand, but necessary if we wish to acquire interior peace.

3. Third consideration: I must entrust myself to God in regard to comprehensive knowledge of myself, of reality, and of the transcendent horizon of all things. Once I so entrust myself, I will be able to gain useful fragments of knowledge, both by inquiry and by deduction, about myself and others.

But my knowledge will always be accompanied by the realization that knowledge of the mystery in its entirety is not granted to us.

Practical Applications

I suggest, as part of the meditation, three practical applications for your lives.

1. The future of the Church is in God's hand, for pastoral plans all depend for their results on countless unforeseeable factors that escape our control and that are known in their totality to God alone.

What is required of us is to apply ourselves humbly to those areas of knowledge that are available to us and to say what courses of action and implementations seem reasonable to us, while accepting the fact that events may betray our expectations, prove us wrong, and force us to revise all our plans.

The greatest attempt to claim knowledge of the totality of facts and to foresee their historical development is to be seen in the totalitarian ideologies that are now collapsing because they have been dramatically belied by circumstances. On our journey as a Church, we can legitimately be influenced by calls for greater rationality, but we must at the same time realize that any rationality is always relative and partial and that its application requires honesty, sincerity, and the ability to respond to situations as we know them, while always keeping in mind the reservation stated by the psalm: "You alone, O Lord, make me lie down in safety" (Ps 4:8).

2. In our pastoral activity we often seek the aid of the social sciences and, more generally, of the scientific knowledge available about our times, our environment, our situation, and the ways in which humankind functions. A contemporary philosopher wrote recently that the social sciences reflect "on the unintended consequences of intentional plans." The reason is that the range of extramental realities and of consequences which reason cannot foresee is vast. The same philosopher contrasted a mindset or mentality that is focused on projects (a mentality that can turn into a claim to program all of reality) and the mentality of pilgrims, which is more open. The pilgrim mentality seeks to accept things as they are, to decide what needs to be done, and then to live with the trust that does not presume to know everything, even about ourselves and whether we are upright and doing what is truly good.

The greater the scope of our responsibilities, the less we should hope to find around us geometric parameters that will ensure the goodness of our actions.

God alone will be able to tell us all that when eternity comes. The important thing is to go forward with the freedom of those who know that God alone is their judge and who endeavor to correct the mistakes of which they become aware, even though they cannot entirely grasp the measure in which these are in fact mistakes.

Such is the mentality Job has great trouble in acquiring. He wants to achieve a clarity about himself, about others, and about God, that leaves no place for shadows. But God rebukes him: "Where were you when I laid the foundations of the earth?" (Job 38:4). What do you know about this, or about anything?

In the matter of personal justice and uprightness Job is finally taught the proper measure (here is the lesson for us). This will emerge in his final statements.

3. I shall risk making an application of what may be called the attitude of loving reverence toward the mystery, an attitude that is fundamental in the Bible and that leads to trust in the covenanted partner: "You have placed your hand on my shoulder, and even if I walk through a dark valley, I shall fear no evil because you are with me."

This attitude can help us in the anxious discussions that go on today about the moral sciences and moral judgments. We live in a situation that is certainly very complex, and it is not always easy to decide what is right when it comes to the great moral decisions (about peace, development, the economy, and so on). I am obviously not referring to individual cases in the here and now but to problems that are cosmic in their scope. It is not possible today to offer, for example, a theory of development that will truly explain all the data of this worldwide problem and not leave out of consideration even a single pocket of misery and suffering. This inability is a reason for anxiety, suffering, and further study. It is not, however, a reason for despair, since the mystery of God guides our universe with all its confusion and absurdity and allows us, moment by moment, to decide on our little tasks, which we carry out in the hope that if we make mistakes, God will forgive us, lead us to a closer union with one another, and make us grow in love.

Only in this spirit is it possible to face up to major moral decisions in situations whose importance and scope we cannot fully grasp.

In this area the Book of Job frees us from our worry about finding completely rational theological answers; it calls into question the attempt to find answers that enclose the boundary problems of the human race within a rational system sus-

ceptible of a secular synthesis. For myself, this is a great
liberation, because theodicy as commonly taught had accustomed me to try to find solutions that would be convinc-
ing to myself and to others. Instead, I am now free, and to
the extent that I have an obligation to look for rational solutions, I do so by seeking historical causes. Giuseppe Dossetti
has some fine pages on this point in the introduction to his
book *Le querce di Montesole*. He looks with unrelenting lucidity
for the historical causes of so many terrible slaughters that have
been inflicted on humankind, as well as for cultural roots in
ideology, roots that can be perceived with a sense of freedom.
If we do not seek solely for abstract rational solutions, we will
be able to involve ourselves in historical reality and see what
is given to us to do here and now.

As we try to answer the question our age poses, Job helps
us to distinguish two lines of thought: one seeks complete,
universal solutions and ends up by plunging us into a series
of questions that form a closed circle and leave us cold, empty,
and dry; the other restores our ability to act with greater love.

This second line of thought fits in with a theological vision
that plunges us more deeply into the Trinitarian mystery as
we push out from the shores of reflection on the one God and
a philosophy of God that is taken over from the Greek tradition. In this vision we surrender to the God of the covenant
and commit ourselves here and now out of love for the people.
This is the only rational solution for those living in this age
of ours.

I would like to add that this is how I myself read the riddle
of the human person today. I am less concerned with my being a priest and bishop than with my being a human person,
that is, one who must render an account of my years of human
life in so tragic and absurd a situation. It is legitimate to let
ourselves be impressed by one or other event which we take
as a symbol (Auschwitz is surely a symbol) of so many evils.
But if we think of what has happened in Cambodia and Arme-
nia and what is now happening in Lebanon, India, and Latin

America, we realize that the issue is not so much the resolution of a situation as it is the possession of a more serious morality and the capacity for using our energies courageously, without indulging straightway in philosophical or theological lamentations. I understand the theology of liberation very well.

Job reaches understanding through trials; by the grace of God, each of us will come to understand the importance of growing above all in abandonment to the mystery, with humility and a listening heart, in reciprocal, patient, persevering love. Then we will find some solutions, perhaps not entirely just and successful, but less unjust and better than those we have at present.

At this point I want to read to you some thoughts of Pope John XXIII in his *Journal of a Soul*, that are in line with my reflections here:

> The more mature I grow in years and experience the more I recognize that the surest way to make myself holy and to succeed in the service of the Holy See lies in the constant effort to reduce everything, principles, aims, position, business, to the utmost simplicity and tranquillity; I must always take care to strip my vines of all useless foliage and spreading tendrils, and concentrate on what is truth, justice and charity, above all charity. Any other way of behaving is nothing but affectation and self-assertion; it soon shows itself in its true colours and become a hindrance and a mockery.
>
> Oh, the simplicity of the Gospel, of the Imitation of Christ, of the *Little Flowers* of St. Francis and of the most exquisite passages in St. Gregory, in his *Moralia* [which is a commentary on the Book of Job]. . . . All the wiseacres of this world, and all cunning minds, including those in Vatican diplomacy, cut such a poor figure in the light of the simplicity and grace shed by this great and fundamental doctrine of Jesus and his saints! This is the surest wisdom, that confounds the learning of this world and, with courtesy and true nobility, is consistent, equally well and even better, with the loftiest achievements in the sphere of science (John XXIII, *Journal of a Soul*, trans. Dorothy White [New York: McGraw-Hill, 1965], 270–71).

Let us humbly pray and ask that we too may be given this outlook, which is not one of submission but rather allows us to walk with courtesy and joy amid the ups and downs of life, and amid all situations and things.

EIGHT

The Struggle for Obedience of the Mind

I am here offering an instruction (not, therefore, a meditation on a passage from the Bible) which will have reference to the Book of Job as a whole and to the meaning this book can have for our Christian lives.

When I chose as the main theme of this retreat the words of Jesus: "You are those who have stood by me in my trials," I wanted to bring to light a particular and at times somewhat neglected aspect of Christian existence: the aspect of conflict and specifically the struggle for the control and obedience of the mind.

This aspect is wonderfully exemplified in Job; the entire book is in fact a great struggle on the part of a human being to make his mind obedient to God.

We shall try therefore to understand, first of all, the meaning of the biblical expression "the obedience of faith." We shall then reflect on the disordered mind, the various kinds of disobedience of mind, and the purification of the mind according to the teaching of the Greek Fathers. Finally, we shall draw some conclusions for ourselves.

"Mary, your mind, your intellect, were purified and obedient from the beginning. After asking but one simple question: 'How shall this

81

be?' you were satisfied and no longer gave entrance to anxieties, second thoughts, and fears. Grant that we may follow in your steps in achieving the pacification of our minds and hearts, so that we may attend with our entire soul and our entire spirit to the service and love of our neighbor, according to our vocation.''

The Obedience of Faith

St. Paul writes: "Through whom," that is, Jesus Christ our Lord, now risen from the dead, "we have received grace and apostleship to bring about the obedience of faith among all the Gentiles for the sake of his name" (Rom 1:5).

The obedience of faith is thus the purpose of Paul's apostolate; it is the reason for the death of Jesus and for sending on the apostles the Holy Spirit who makes them able precisely to win from others this obedience of faith. The purpose of the Church, of the Christian mission is no different: to obtain from every rational creature the obedience of faith to the mystery of God, to the kerygma, to the proclamation of salvation. The theme is a central one throughout the New Testament. It is not an accident that in its closing doxology the Letter to the Romans repeats the point with which it began: "Now to God who is able to strengthen you according to my gospel and the proclamation of Jesus Christ, according to the revelation of the mystery that was kept secret for long ages but is now disclosed, and through the prophetic writings is made known to all the Gentiles, according to the command of the eternal God, to bring about *the obedience of faith*—to the only wise God, through Jesus Christ, to whom be the glory forever! Amen" (Rom 16:25-27).

The same idea finds expression in the Letter to the Hebrews where it is said of the Son of God that "having been made perfect, he became the source of eternal salvation for all who obey him" (Heb 5:9).

Jesus becomes our savior through the basic action called "the obedience of faith."

Even the patriarchs of old were saved through obedience and hearing: "By faith Abraham obeyed when he was called to set out for a place that he was to receive as an inheritance; and he set out, not knowing where he was going" (Heb 11:8). We can imagine Abraham journeying toward the first stopping place on his pilgrimage, not knowing what his destination was to be. What a tumult of questions must have broken out in his mind! He certainly had no easy answer to such questions as: Who is impelling me to do this? Is it the right thing to do? Why did I not stay where I was?

The obedience of faith is not given once and for all in a single indivisible act; rather it marks the beginning of a struggle against all worldly temptations to disobedience, self-sufficiency, presumptuousness, and all the thoughts characteristic of what the scriptures call the carnal or physical or natural human being who, as Paul tells us, always has countless arguments against faith.

The Disorderly Mind

The obedience of faith supposes the conquest of all that introduces disorder into the mind: contrary or troubling illusions that resist the journey of faith and argue against it or ridicule it or call it into question, or that would like to interpret it differently and challenge it. These illusions are legion and create bedlam, as the unclean spirits say of themselves in the episode of the demoniac at Gerasa (Mk 5:1f.).

Those who want to undertake the journey of faith are well aware of this. Every human being is subject to these countless troublesome and crisscrossing ideas that, like parasites or grasshoppers or gnats, keep buzzing around and prevent concentration on the fundamental duty. Those who do not attempt a spiritual life are not aware of them but live by impressions from the books and newspapers they read, the sounds they hear, rumors, and television, moving from one to another of these things in a continual maelstrom of imaginations, fantasies, and desires, switching from each vision to the next, like people who watch program after program on the television and are constantly subject to some new stimulus.

Disorder in thoughts is, it may be said, a constant situation in human life, even if we are not aware of it. We become aware of it when we begin to cultivate silence and regular meditation, for then we are assailed by a throng of useless, empty, disordered thoughts, and the struggle against them can be a real hidden martyrdom, a real penance that can be a substitute for a good many other, external penances. But the struggle is also a requisite for mental health, because those who succeed in disciplining the world of fantasies, feelings, desires, fears, anticipations, escapes into the future, and nostalgias achieve a degree of interior good health. Otherwise human beings are constantly tossed about by opposing feelings amid which they are unable to set a course, and their moods change quickly as they react for which they cannot account even to themselves.

The struggle against the disorderly mind is one of the most important activities of those who desire to obey God and abandon themselves to his action.

Various Forms of Disobedience of the Mind

I would like to specify at least a few of the numerous ways in which the mind can be disobedient. Many thoughts are merely bothersome; we call them distractions: they come and go, but do not militate directly against obedience, although they always have the capability of weakening the powers of the spirit.

Not infrequently, however, the thoughts become forms—even if only implicit or hidden—of real disobedience to faith. Job is a constant example of this. If we reread the Book of Job with this in mind, we see that as Job and his friends speak, they voice a chaotic multiplicity of ideas, many of which tend to disobedience. We ourselves have experience of these:

thoughts, for example, which whirl around in our heads and make us rebel against the situation in which we find ourselves; a refusal to accept ourselves, our physical state, our family, our history; a refusal to accept society. We are indeed bound to combat the evils of society, but if we daydream and conjure up different, unreal circumstances, this prevents us from loving, serving, and contributing to the improvement of the world, because we constantly have before our minds a situation different from the real one.

Or again, we refuse to accept that we are sinners, that we have erred. How often we are tormented by self-justification; especially when we are criticized, justly or unjustly, our minds produce a lengthy theory by which to justify ourselves, and we review the situation over and over in order to tell ourselves that others did not understand us and that we were in the right.

Job also teaches us the danger of refusing to accept our ignorance of who we are and whether or not we are upright; the danger inherent in an unqualified need to define ourselves, to know ourselves down to our very roots. There is, moreover, a kind of psychological self-analysis or self-psychoanalysis that reinforces this desire for self-knowledge; I want to possess myself consciously down to my depths and therefore I engage in an endless investigation of dreams, fantasies, nervous tics, and unconscious gestures in the hope of discovering the secret part of myself that is difficult to grasp.

From such thoughts as these one surely passes eventually to thoughts involving a more direct disobedience: the refusal to accept God. This is, in the final analysis, the great temptation that runs through the Book of Job. Job does accept God, and this is his great act of faith, but his mind is constantly tempted to refuse; he is tempted to despair and to resignation in the bad sense: ''I no longer believe in anything, I accept nothing, I no longer desire anything.''

Such is the twisting course of our thoughts: they usually present themselves as harmless; they fill our minds during the early hours of the morning; they assail us at times when we are not very busy, suddenly invading our minds so that when we take up our tasks we feel sad, tired, and weak without knowing why. The fact is that we have not carefully disciplined our thoughts, we have not put a halt to them; as a result, feelings of exaltation or resentment, attraction or depression or vexation at ourselves or others have entered into us without our adverting to it, and then we have encouraged them.

I might also mention sensual fantasies, desires, all the reveries that make their way in, even surreptitiously, and leave us somewhat empty, with little attraction to prayer and little devotion to Mass and the recitation of the breviary. We do not understand the reason for our emptiness; it is in fact simply that we have let ourselves be amused, without adverting to it, by a string of undisciplined thoughts that have finally enfeebled us.

The discovery of this difficult interior world is part of the spiritual journey and leads us to take on a continuous and most wearisome struggle.

Purification of the Mind According to the Fathers

If we bear all this in mind we have a key for reading intelligently a large number of texts from the mainstream literature of the Eastern Fathers and especially from monastic literature. The *Philokalia* deals extensively with this theme: the struggle for discipline of the mind, the thoughts, the sentiments of the heart. When monks enter upon the solitary life, they are called to confront primarily their own interior world, and their lives become a struggle to reduce it to obedience.

In this regard, the volumes of the *Philokalia* are rich in spiritual and psychological wisdom; they enable us to participate in a millennial tradition of mental discipline. The very titles of the various works in the *Philokalia* are expressive: *On Guarding the Intellect*, by Isaiah the Solitary; *Outline Teaching on Asceticism and Stillness in the Solitary Life*, by Evagrios the Solitary ("stillness" translates *hesychia* and means the tranquillity enjoyed by those who possess their own minds, that is, possess the interior peace which is regarded as the ideal of the monastic life and for which monks struggle throughout their lives); *Texts on Discrimination in Respect of Passions and Thoughts*, by the same Evagrios; *On the Eight Vices*, by Cassian. Cassian's treatise brings to light, unmasks, and provides weapons against all those thoughts that weaken human beings; for with these thoughts the passions also come into play, so that Cassian's treatise goes to the very root of the heart.

From among so many interesting passages I shall read to you one of Evagrios on discernment. In the picturesque style that is typical of the Desert Fathers, he writes: "There is a demon, known as the deluder, who visits the brethren especially at dawn, and leads the intellect about from city to city, from village to village, from house to house, pretending that no passions are aroused through such visits." The demon thus presents itself as harmless when it causes the solitary to think of this or that person.

> But then the intellect goes on to meet and talk with old acquaintances at greater length, and so allows its own state to be corrupted by those it encounters. Little by little it falls away from the knowledge of God and holiness, and forgets its calling. Therefore the solitary must watch this demon, noting where he comes from and where he ends up; for this demon does not make this long circuit without purpose and at random, but because he wishes to corrupt the state of the solitary, so that his intellect, over-excited by all this wandering, and intoxicated by its many meetings, may immediately fall prey to the demons of unchastity, anger or dejection—the demons that above all others destroy its inherent brightness (*Texts on Discrimination* . . . 8, in *The Philokalia* I, trans. G. E. H. Palmer, Philip Sherrard, and Kallistos Ware [Boston: Faber and Faber, 1979], 43).

I think the process whereby the mind is corrupted is clearly outlined in this passage.

Suggestions

Finally, I shall offer some conclusions.

1. It is legitimate, to a certain point, that we should try to use reason in order to extricate ourselves from the whirl of thoughts that assail us. We are instinctively led to give a logical answer to each of them because they often manifest themselves to us as questions.

2. There is, however, a limit. As our sensitivities grow, we become aware in fact that the questions are really not quieted with an answer but continue to depress the spirit. Then we must become aware of the struggle and bring into play the disciplined attitude proper to those seeking *hesychia*, the orderly control of their own minds. We do this in three ways:

a) The first is by courageously cutting short the whirl of thoughts, even if it means repeating this decision over and over again. As soon as we realize that the thoughts are not constructive, even though they seem reasonable, but rather weaken the mind, we must immediately cut them short. There are many who, if they had done this in time, would have been spared many nervous breakdowns, disappointments, resentments already too long cultivated, and many fatigues.

Interior decisiveness is therefore very important.

b) The second way, which is suggested by *The Imitation of Christ*, among others, is simple; we often forget it, but it is truly efficacious. It is to "do what you are doing" (*age quod agis*), to give yourself wholly to what you are doing, thus turning your senses into helpers. If you are reading a book, then feel it in your hand, feel its weight, focus your eyes on the words one after another, try to attend to them with the aid of the very printed letters themselves. In like manner, if you are singing, sing with all your heart; if you are writing, write with all your energy; if you are walking, walk with all your strength. Do not let yourself be made captive by parasitic thoughts that seek, by means of resentments, animosities, fears, and anxieties, to control your action. This may seem overly simple a means, but it is most useful, and there are even schools of psychology based on the practice; the theory is that an ordered self-consciousness has as its starting point the sensible perception of realities directly at hand and then orders the sequence of thoughts along a direct line, without continually diverging to the right or the left.

c) The third suggestion, often given by the Greek Fathers, especially in the course of the monastic tradition, is the Jesus prayer. This prayer consists of carrying the mind into the heart and therefore of not allowing the mind to spread out in the thicket of thoughts, but instead focusing it completely and in an affective way on the person of Jesus. The prayer of the heart has a technique of its own, one that is perhaps not very suitable for us Westerners but that in the Greek and Russian Churches has led its practitioners to great heights of mysticism.

But we too have versions of the prayer of the heart: the Rosary, for example, when properly recited, tends to pacify the mind by concentrating it on some basic words and images; the Way of the Cross gives rise to sentiments and affections focused on Jesus; ejaculations and psalm verses often repeated can become a prayer of the heart. Gradually the multiplicity of thoughts undergoes a simplification and a reduction to unity. The several practices mentioned are ways that can help us recover that interior unity—amid distraction and the discontinuity often caused by the multiplicity of activities—which finds in the Jesus prayer its privileged point of reference.

As a result of my experiences in India, where I became acquainted at close hand with Hindu asceticism and the ways followed by many young people in their search for gurus or spiritual masters, I came to realize that there too the ideal is to achieve self-possession and unity, not by the paths of rational, possessive logic but by self-surrender. In India they speak of self-emptying, of abandonment to the void. For us the abandonment is to the ineffable mystery in which we are immersed and which, being closer to me than I am to myself, is present in the depths of our heart. As a result, we can find it at every moment—day or night, in sickness or in health, in sadness or in joy— and achieve a profound unity within ourselves.

The Jesus prayer is within the reach of all and yet it leads us into profound mysteries; it is compatible with, and adaptable too, all situations and can be practiced even by those who have many commitments and perhaps little time for prolonged and intense prayer. We must, of course, also recognize from experience that it is not possible to practice the Jesus prayer or any affective prayer of the heart in an effective way during the activities of the day, unless we set aside some intense periods of serious prayer and silence.

3. A final observation has to do with the "anger of the intellect," an expression I borrow from Isaiah the Solitary. "There is among the passions an anger of the intellect, and this anger is in accordance with nature." It is therefore a good anger, since in the Greek tradition "in accordance with nature" means "in accordance with God," in accordance with the way God made things. Without anger a man cannot attain purity: he has to feel angry with all that is sown in him by the enemy." If persons patiently endure the invasion of a whirl of thoughts and do not perceive these as hostile, they are not living according to the truth and will never achieve interior purity.

> When Job felt this anger he reviled his enemies, calling them "dishonourable men of no repute, lacking everything good, whom I would not consider fit to live with the dogs that guard my flocks" (cf. Job 30:1, 4. LXX). . . .
>
> If you find yourself hating your fellow men and resist this hatred, and you see that it grows weak and withdraws, do not rejoice in your heart; for this withdrawal is a trick of the evil spirits. They are preparing a second attack worse than the first; they have left their troops behind the city and ordered them to remain there. If you go out to attack them, they will flee before you in weakness. But if your heart is then elated because you have driven them away, and you leave the city, some of them will attack you from the rear while the rest will stand their

ground in front of you; and your wretched soul will be caught between them with no means of escape. The city is prayer. Resistance is rebuttal through Christ Jesus. The foundation is incensive power (*On Guarding the Intellect* 1-2, in *The Philokalia* I, 22).

Isaiah the Solitary says, therefore, that we must get angry at everything that tries to destroy and trouble us, so that we may attain to a strong interior discipline which alone makes it possible to live even amid continual changes in the situation around us and in our own spiritual situation. We must also, however, keep our eyes fixed on the Lord Jesus, the Prince of Peace who reigns in our hearts above and beyond all the ups and downs of human life.

This is the obedience of the mind which Job attained only after lengthy toil and very painful distress.

May the Lord grant that we quickly reach this goal which is so important for our life and our pastoral service.

NINE

The Ineffable Justice of God

(Homily for Wednesday of the Twentieth Week of Ordinary
   Time)
(Readings: Judges 9:6-15; Matthew 20:1-16)

"Grant, Lord, that we may live in an intense way the Eucharistic Communion, which has no boundaries but extends to all whom we know and love and all who have been entrusted to our care; to the sick and the suffering; to all the Churches, the Pope, the dioceses, all the bishops, all the missions, and all of humankind's most painful situations. Grant, Father, that we may live in your presence as representatives of the human race, thus carrying out our priestly service within the broadest possible horizon."

The first reading, from the Book of Judges (9:6-15), provides us with the first example in the Bible of a parable, that is, a fictional story. In this case, it contains a very transparently antimonarchical, antiauthoritarian message.

The story is the first example of the mistrust of the monarchy that will appear clearly in the first Book of Samuel, when the question arises of giving Israel a king. It is an expression of the apprehension felt about entrusting the destinies of all the people to a single individual.

The parable brings on the scene various trees that are useful to human beings and are here possessed of intelligence, reason, and uprightness. These trees are benefactors of the human race, such as the olive tree and the vine, but they are unwilling to consider taking responsibility for others, for they have, as they say, a task that is more important and one which only they can perform.

The tree that is willing to accept the responsibility is one that produces no fruit and is useless: the bramble.

As applied to human beings, the parable is saying that those who are truly astute stick to their own job and remain within their own field. It is those who lack real understanding who accept responsibility for others and who, when they accept it, become pretentious, vain, proud, and cruel, like the bramble.

We have here a very negative description of the role of power in history. To some extent it certainly corresponds to reality; how often it happens, in politics for example, that people truly upright, qualified, and able refuse to become involved, while those who would do better to refuse agree to become politicians.

Beyond the human wisdom contained in the story there is a deeper, biblical teaching: human destinies are in God's hand and it is not good to entrust them to a human being. "You alone, O Lord, make me lie down in safety" (Ps 4:8).

The parable thus gives voice to distrust and a fear that, if the destinies of some human beings are placed in the hands of others, there will be abuses of power and forms of oppression unworthy of the people of God. The entire history recounted in the Books of Kings shows how well founded this fear was. The fear makes itself felt throughout the history of salvation, where it is constantly said that while some persons are set in charge of others, they are but shepherds of the flock, subordinate to the one supreme shepherd, Jesus. It is he who has full and complete responsibility for believers; all others are subordinate to him, they are his agents and caretakers. They must see to proper order and progress, while remaining aware that it is in the Lord that the people of God hope and trust.

It is very important that we learn to interpret properly all human authorities, including those in the Church, and be aware that the honor given to them is always referred beyond them to him who alone is truly responsible for our souls, him who is the sole head of the Church: the Lord Jesus Christ, on whom all other authority depends. He alone is worthy to open the book, sealed with seven seals, that contains the secrets of the kingdom of God. For he is Lamb that was slain, the one who gave himself even to death for us.

Everything we do is related to Christ the Lord and his power which alone is inherently legitimate; all other forms of authority are but limited participations in this service which is the very life of Jesus.

The parable which Jesus tells in the gospel (Matt 20:1-16) continues along the line of the preceding reflections; we might say it continues the line taken in the Book of Job.

Instead of Job we have the laborers in the vineyard, some of whom grumble because they want the landowner to practice a strict justice. The question, of course, is: What is true justice? The landowner says he will give the workers what is right, but the latter claim, to some extent, that justice must be a matter of strict proportionality, so that it can be determined in advance on a calculator; there is to be no room for kindness, love, mercy, or the infinity that marks God's plan.

Job needs to be converted from a very strong and lively, but univocal and geometric understanding of justice that seeks to comprehend the self and God within this changeless and unchallengeable framework. In fact, however, God is a Trinity of love; he is a God of surprises; his relationship to us is one of indescribable tenderness and brings into play a mysterious love that both reveals and veils itself and manifests itself in ever new forms.

Human beings are therefore called upon to act according to the justice of God: the justice characteristic of his triune being, which is marked by devotion, self-giving, inventiveness, creativity, and a goodness astonishingly greater than we can possibly imagine.

During these days of retreat, we too are summoned to conversion, so that we will no longer conceive the God of revelation by means of ideas which we superimpose on him and in terms of which we judge him, even if these be the loftiest of ideas, such as justice and charity. We must come to know the God of the covenant as he really is in his overflowing life, a life brimming over with love and mercy: the God who amid deepest darkness is working out his luminous plans.

The laborers in the vineyard, Job, and each of us are asked to trust ourselves to the mystery of God.

We pray that we may walk this path, aided by adoration of the Eucharistic mystery, before which we feel bewildered each time we celebrate and renew it and hold in our hands the body and blood of Christ. We are bewildered because this mystery cannot be comprehended by our limited concepts but transcends in love all our anticipations and calculations and even our loftiest ideas about the mystery of an infinite God who stoops to his poor, limited creatures.

TEN

Three Ways of Struggling with God

As we endeavor to understand the enigma of Job or, more accurately, to enter a little more deeply into the mystery of the most high, unknowable, merciful and just, sovereign and inscrutable, thrice Holy God, we must bear in mind that the Book of Job is part of the Scriptures and that its message is therefore to be understood in the context of the biblical message as a whole.

For this reason I suggest that as we continue our reading we also look to other pages of the Old and New Testaments, and that we do so from three points of view. These I will call, using somewhat pretentious terms, the anthropological, Christological, and Trinitarian points of view.

We have seen Job struggling against disorder in the mind; all of his suffering is meant to cleanse his mind of the multiplicity of thoughts that seem reasonable, correct, and logical but that in the end are unsound. His ultimate action is surrender to the mystery.

In this struggle against disorder in the mind Job is also struggling with God. Like Jacob in that mysterious story which is the prototype of all struggles with God in history and in spirituality, Job wants to be blessed, justified, and declared upright; he wants to obtain what he desires.

The theme of struggle with God is an inexhaustible one. Perhaps we do not often come to grips with it because (we think) it has to do with Christian mysticism. But it does have meaning for us, and we should delve into it.

I suggest, therefore, that we reflect on three episodes from the anthropological point of view:

- Chapter 10 of Job: "Address of the creature against the Creator";
- Chapter 2 of St. John (vv. 1–12);
- Chapter 25 of St. Matthew (vv. 21–28), with the parallel passage in Mark (7:24-30).

Complaint of the Creature against the Creator (Job 10)

"Job seems to be introducing a kind of imaginary address to be delivered before a hypothetical high court of justice where God is also present" (Ravasi, *Giobbe*, 408). The address may be divided into the following sections:

- Vv. 1-2, introduction to the complaint.

I loathe my life;
  I will give free utterance to my complaint;
  I will speak in the bitterness of my soul.
I will say to God, Do not condemn me;
  let me know why you contend against me.

With these words Job engages in close combat with God.

- Vv. 3-7: the complaint begins with five questions addressed to the enemy.

Earlier we heard God questioning Job. Now it is Job who bombards God with rhetorical questions aiming at overcoming him.

Does it seem good to you to oppress,
  to despise the work of your hands
  and favor the schemes of the wicked?

> Do you have eyes of flesh?
> Do you see as humans do?
> Are your days like the days of mortals,
> or your years like human years,
> that you seek out my iniquity
> and search for my sin,
> although you know that I am not guilty,
> and there is no one to deliver out of your hand?

God's goodness is being challenged here: Why do you deal with me in a way that does not befit you? Why do you not treat me with kindness?

• Vv. 8-12: questions are succeeded by a moving peroration, as in an advocate's address when he pleads for the mercy of the court:

> Your hands fashioned and made me;
> and now you turn and destroy me.
> Remember that you fashioned me like clay;
> and will you turn me to dust again?
> Did you not pour me out like milk
> and curdle me like cheese?
> You clothed me with skin and flesh,
> and knit me together with bones and sinews.
> You have granted me life and steadfast love,
> and your care has preserved my spirit.

Although no explicit mention is made of it, we can find in Job's words a reference to the mystery of the covenant: you created me, you made me your own, I am yours: do not forget your creature; stay near me and do not abandon me.

• Vv. 13-17: the peroration is followed by charges against him who acts like an enemy: "Yet these things you hid in your heart; I know that this was your purpose" (v. 13).

The charge is a serious one, and the *Jerusalem Bible* in its note on the verse (in the Italian edition) has some trouble explaining it: "Job's lament conveys a tragic truth. Making spontaneous use of their own freedom, human beings should be able to live in peace with God and harmony with other beings and things. In fact, however, they feel dependent on a mysterious, demanding will that leaves them uncertain about themselves and God, tests their consciences, and denies them the assurances on which they would like to rely. Job evokes, in negative terms, the drama of faith" (p. 1055).

This note perhaps reads more into the passage than is present in it, but Job's words do express something of the mystery of human beings faced with an uncertainty they would like to resolve:

> If I sin, you watch me,
>   and do not acquit me of my iniquity.
> If I am wicked, woe to me!
>   If I am righteous, I cannot lift up my head,
> for I am filled with disgrace
>   and look upon my affliction.
> Bold as a lion you hunt me;
>   you repeat your exploits against me.
> You renew your witnesses against me,
>   and increase your vexation toward me;
>   you bring fresh troops against me.

God is thus seen as a cruel wild beast who will not leave this poor fellow in peace.

• Vv. 18-22: another shift takes place here from aggressiveness to petition that appeals to the affective side of the divine mystery.

> Why did you bring me forth from the womb?
>   Would that I had died before any eye had seen me,
> and were as though I had not been,
>   carried from the womb to the grave.
> Are not the days of my life few?
>   Let me alone, that I may find a little comfort

> before I go, never to return,
>> to the land of gloom and deep darkness,
> the land of gloom and chaos,
>> where light is like darkness.

In this chapter Job gives voice to his loneliness, his uncertainty, his suffering at not being heard; in addition, as happens to one with a strong inferiority complex, he becomes irritated and struggles to obtain what he wants from the One whom he thinks can and should give it to him. He speaks with the anger of one who is not sure of himself and yet claims his rights.

Here, then, is a struggle with God, but it is still to a great extent a struggle with himself, with his uncontrolled thoughts, with the sense of inferiority that assails him, with the insecurity that eats at him interiorly and which he seeks to shrug off with threatening words. It may be that persons who are most aggressive verbally are the weakest and most fragile and that they attack furiously because they are afraid of not getting what they want.

Mary's Struggle with Jesus (John 2)

Job's is one way of struggling with God; I would like to contrast with it the way in which the Mother of Jesus struggled at the wedding feast of Cana. Mary thinks she should receive what she wants, but she cannot be absolutely certain of success. She therefore bends all her efforts to wresting from her Son what she wants of him.

The struggle is expressed in a restrained and veiled way, but it is nonetheless a struggle with God.

Mary begins by acting as the couple's advocate with Jesus and explaining their situation to him in a very brief but urgent plea: "When the wine gave out, the mother of Jesus said to him, 'They have no wine' " (Jn 2:3).

Her words are filled with sorrow: Now that you and I are here, how can we fail to help these people by preventing a humiliation that will cast a lifelong shadow over them and be a sign of misfortune for their marriage? This is a marvelous statement, taking a negative fact and confronting Jesus with a situation that needs remedying.

Jesus, however, seems to leave Mary isolated. "And Jesus said to her, 'Woman, what concern is that to you and to me? My hour has not yet come'" (v. 4). Whatever be the precise meaning of Jesus' question, it is certain at least that he is not welcoming and encouraging her but distancing himself.

Mary receives no help; she is alone, like Job. Then she makes a truly heroic gesture of trust, for it includes others as well as herself. She calls the servants and says to them: "Do whatever he tells you" (v. 5). By this public action the Mother of Jesus forces his assent. She acts in this way because she does not have any feeling of inferiority or fear or weakness that would make her grow angry or cry out; rather she is certain of the covenant. Therefore she trustingly surrenders both herself and the servants to the power of Jesus, which she is sure will provide, though she does not know how.

We may note that her surrender continues until the decisive moment, even if her name is not mentioned again in the story. She continues to trust even though her Son is apparently acting against her expectations. What we are told about the six jars, each holding two or three barrelfuls, which Jesus orders to be filled with water, seems, at first sight, alien to what might be expected; it is as though Jesus were saying: If there is no wine, let them be satisfied with water! The impression is given that Jesus does not take his mother's request seriously. Everything that happens afterward, and even the joy of the evangelist as he proclaims that Jesus worked his first miracle at Cana (see v. 11), is due to Mary. For she, as she struggles and urgently asks and enters into a situation of need, retains the confidence of one who has by now won out in the struggle for obedience of mind.

In our own struggles with God we may find ourselves to be somewhere between Job and Mary. We must strive to grow closer to Mary, as far as this is possible for us on our spiritual journey, by achieving the obedience of mind that is the fundamental attitude of creatures in relation to God.

The Struggle of the Canaanite Woman (Matt 15:21-28)

The story of the struggle of the Canaanite woman with Jesus is a very beautiful one that closely parallels John's story of the wedding feast at Cana.

This is a woman who knows that she does not belong to the chosen people and therefore has no rights and can entertain but small hope. Nonetheless she endeavors with her entire being to win from Jesus what she wants of him.

"A Canaanite woman from that region [Tyre and Sidon] came out and started shouting, 'Have mercy on me, Lord, Son of David; my daughter is tormented by a demon' " (v. 22). Observe how powerful her plea is. By calling him "Son of David," she appeals to Jesus' family roots and to the power of the messianic promises that rest on him. She also calls him "Lord," a title that opens into the mystery of the divine omnipotence. She uses words that stir compassion ("Have mercy on me"), and she describes her daughter's suffering. All this is contained in her sorrowful and effective plea.

Note, too, how wonderfully the mother identifies with her daughter: "Have mercy *on me*": it is my daughter who suffers, but I suffer with her, and therefore it is I who ask you for mercy.

And yet Jesus does not listen to her; he says not even a word in reply (see v. 23).

The Canaanite woman experiences a piercing sense of loneliness and rejection, but she only struggles more intensely to obtain what she wants. In order to succeed, she somehow gets at the disciples, who "came and urged him, saying, 'Send her away, for she keeps shouting after us,' " as though she were embarrassing them.

She meets with a second rejection when "he answered, 'I was sent only to the lost sheep of the house of Israel' " (v. 24). This answer is apparently decisive, since Jesus is defining the limits of his mission.

If the woman were caught in the same disobedience of mind which Job experienced, she would at this point have begun to curse a plan of God that did not transcend the narrow confines of a proud and self-centered people, incapable of paying heed to their neighbors. She would have descended to insults and aggressiveness.

Instead, the woman kneels before the Lord and says: "Lord, help me" (v. 25). The struggle continues, but in the realm of love, affection, and mercy, for the Canaanite woman is now certain of Jesus' mercy, beyond what his words might allow her to presume.

Her insight enables her to say, as it were: I know you and I know that you can help me and want to help me; I know that you are acting in this way to test me. She experiences Jesus' answer as a testing and is thus able to understand it as a purification of her faith. She therefore receives his answer humbly and peacefully, but with undiminished resolve.

She is now rejected for a third time, and in a very harsh way: "It is not fair to take the children's food and throw it to the dogs" (v. 26). The words sound like a chauvinist insult, and as calculated to stir rebellion, anger, and incredible interior irritation. The struggle between God and the woman has reached its climax. We are here at a profound mystical level, and it is extraordinary to see how the woman, possessed of an absolute obedience of mind, does not curse Jesus or rail at him, but manages to be humorous, so free and confident does she feel: "Yes, Lord, yet even the dogs eat the crumbs that fall from their masters' table" (v. 27).

The answer is incomparably sublime and points to a person who, despite the words she has heard, truly believes in Jesus, in the mercy of God, and in the universality of the covenant. Thus the woman emerges victorious.

Jesus wants to be conquered. The mystery of the struggle with God resides in the fact that the angel is content to have been overcome by Jacob (see Gen 32:23ff.). As a rabbinic moral fable says: God is satisfied to be overcome and conquered by his children.

The exultation which Jesus feels bursts into words: "Woman, great is your faith! Let it be done for you as you wish" (v. 28). Her faith is great indeed because it has understood the heart of Christ despite all the veils behind which the Lord hid his love in order to raise faith to a heroic level.

It is worth noting the parallel verse in Mark, for it is perhaps even more enlightening: "For saying that, you may go—the demon has left your daughter" (Mk 7:29). According to this, the woman's words were powerful, and Jesus rejoices because the miracle was not as it were solely his but was also due to the power of human faith. Jesus has won because he has succeeded in bringing the Canaanite woman to an unparalleled level of faith, a faith like that of Abraham. The woman, too, has conquered because she has made Jesus show himself to be truly divine.

I have sometimes asked myself what would have happened if in response to Jesus' behavior the Canaanite woman had begun to rail against him. The Lord certainly does not work miracles for those who reject him, but I think that in this case he would have distinguished various attitudes.

If the woman had railed like Job, therefore with faith and a desire to seek God, I think Jesus would have granted her request. But the Canaanite woman would have been lost to us. If our Lady had railed, Jesus would have granted her request, for he would have seen what was truly at work in her attitude. But Mary would have fallen short of the profound peace of mind which she in fact achieved.

It is we who destroy ourselves. Jesus is always motivated by love and mercy in his dealing with those who show themselves eager to receive him.

Our Ability to Struggle with God

As we read and apply the three stories to ourselves, we should try to profit from them chiefly through affective contemplation.

How capable are we of struggling with God? Are we among those who are easily cast down? who feel forgotten and abandoned, even if we do not admit as much to ourselves but nonetheless feel this way in the depths of our consciousness?

Or do we try to follow the example of Mary and the Canaanite woman, who challenge God and advance from faith to faith in the struggle of life; who accept the difficult moments and also accept darkness as the depth from which they must cry? For it is here that God tests, as by fire, their faith and the selflessness of their surrender, so that this may find the unrestricted expression that represents the high point of every human journey ever since Abraham.

We may see here a kind of synthesis of the entire history of salvation. Human beings, created by divine love and summoned to be tested, are unable to accept the challenge of faith; their fundamental sin is to be unable to trust in him and rely on the guidance he gives in his word. Then God restores the human race by the way of faith, beginning with Abraham. Thus faith is purified as it travels down through all the great personages of the Old Testament; it takes on a special enigmatic yet exemplary form in Job; finally, it reaches its high point in the faith of Mary, the faith of the saints of the new covenant, and, ultimately, the self-surrender of Jesus to the Father. Jesus is the human being who achieves total, full, and complete self-surrender, even in the moment when it seems that the Father is abandoning him to utter darkness and isolation.

All the persons I have mentioned—Abraham, Jacob, Job, Mary, the Canaanite woman—come together, as it were, in Jesus, whom the Father abandons and who surrenders himself to the Father. Together they provide us with a unified vision of the salvation in which we are called upon to encounter the mystery of God in our daily struggles.

ELEVEN

Three Exemplars of Obedience of the Mind

Always with the Book of Job in mind, I have chosen some passages of Scripture that will aid us in reflection of a Christological kind.

We have already gone into the importance of obedience of the mind; I shall now illustrate the theme with three concrete cases:

Abraham (Gen 22);

Job (Job 40–42);

Jesus (Mk 14).

With a view to the prayer for grace that precedes our meditation, I have sought inspiration in a passage of the Letter to the Hebrews that might be considered a summary of an entire retreat:

> Therefore, since we are surrounded by so great a cloud of witnesses, let us also lay aside every weight and the sin that clings so closely, and let us run with perseverance the race that is set before us, looking to Jesus the pioneer and perfecter of our faith, who for the sake of the joy that was set before him endured the cross, disregarding its shame, and has taken his seat at the right hand of the throne of God. Consider him who endured such hostility against himself from sinners, so that you may not grow weary or lose heart (Heb 12:1-3).

Jesus, the pioneer and perfecter of our faith, has passed through the great trial. This reached its climax in the shame of the cross, to which he was subjected as he endured the great hostility of sinners. His example spurs us on to run perseveringly along the way that stretches before us and to put aside the weight and the sin that clings to us. For we are surrounded by a great cloud of witnesses: all the saints of the Old and New Covenants, especially those mentioned in the Letter to the Hebrews, Abraham among them (see Heb 11).

"Grant, O Jesus, that above all else we may keep our eyes fixed on you. It is from you that our faith comes; it is you who bring it to completion. You endured trials before us, you lead us, you will not allow us to stray from the way.

"Grant that we may contemplate you with great love and be able to find strength and joy in following you, even when we face difficult choices."

The Obedience of Abraham

"After these things God tested Abraham. He said to him, 'Abraham!' " (Gen 22:1). We are at the climactic moment of Abraham's life, a moment which the entire tradition will look upon as one of profound mystery and drama, even reading it symbolically to refer to Christ on the cross and the relationship of the Son with the Father "who did not withhold his own Son" (Rom 8:32).

God, then, puts Abraham to the test. He calls him by name and commands him: " 'Take your son, your only son Isaac, whom you love, and go to the land of Moriah and offer him there as a burnt offering on one of the mountains that I will show you.' So Abraham rose early in the morning, saddled his donkey, and took two of his young men with him, and his son Isaac; he cut the wood for the burnt offering, and set out and went to the place in the distance that God had shown him" (vv. 1b-3). We are surprised by the terseness of the story, which seems to regard the whole affair as obvious: God commands, Abraham obeys, rising early in the morning and taking to the road.

Yet it is easy to imagine the conflict that raged in Abraham's soul: the thoughts and objections and feelings of rebellion that assailed him, the repugnance he felt while performing outwardly simple actions, as though he were simply going for a walk in the country. We are surprised that the biblical story does not mention any of this, does not refer to the dramatic struggle in Abraham's soul. The Letter to the Hebrews does speak of it: "By faith Abraham, when put to the test, offered up Isaac. He who had received the promises was ready to offer up his only son, of whom he had been told, 'It is through Isaac that descendants shall be named for you'" (Heb 11:17-18). These verses express, in a summary way, the entire interior battle that Abraham had to fight: Why have you given me such a command as this? Me, who am heir to the promises but have now been deceived, after finding delight in the promise of the descendants for whom I have waited for years? If only I had more than one son! But to take Isaac, my only son, the very one of whom you said to me: "It is through Isaac that descendants shall be named for you"!

On the one hand, Abraham struggles as he feels within his mind the tumult of objections—so easy, so reasonable, so logical, like those of Job. On the other, as the Letter to the Hebrews says, "He considered the fact that God is able even to raise someone from the dead—and figuratively speaking, he did receive him back" (Heb 11:19).

Abraham is able to practice obedience of the mind because he trusts beyond all trust, hopes against all hope, as Paul puts it in a powerful phrase.

As Abraham walks along in silence, trying to repress, to control the throng of tormenting thoughts, his son, in all simplicity and candor, asks the question that should not have been asked and that could well have brought into the open the interior storm that Abraham is experiencing. "Isaac said to his father Abraham, 'Father!' And he said, 'Here I am, my son.' He said, 'The fire and the wood are here, but where is the lamb for a burnt offering?' '' Abraham feels as though his heart is being pierced, but he replies: ''God himself will provide the lamb for a burnt offering, my son'' (Gen 22:7-8).

This is indeed obedience of the mind: the surrender, beyond what any evidence could demand, to the God who is greater than we, who is omniscient and omnipotent and provides for everything. In fact, the name of the place was henceforth to be ''The Lord will provide'': ''. . . as it is said to this day, 'On the mount of the Lord it shall be provided' '' (v. 14).

This, then, is a first, dramatic example of obedience of the mind, that is, of homage paid to a mystery whose intelligibility we do not grasp but whose power we experience within us.

It is for this reason that Abraham is the founder of our faith.

The End of Job's Journey

Job has indulged in a great deal of wild talk, but at the end of God's first discourse, he finds words that show he has attained to obedience.

And the Lord said to Job:
''Shall a faultfinder contend with the Almighty?
Anyone who argues with God must respond.''
Then Job answered the Lord:
''See, I am of small account; what shall I answer you?
I lay my hand on my mouth.
I have spoken once, and I will not answer;
twice, but will proceed no further'' (Jb 40:1-2).

This first reply of Job is an acknowledgment that the world, the mystery of history, and the mystery of each individual human being are contained within a greater mystery which is beyond our control.

There now follows God's second discourse (40:6-41), which has caused rivers of ink to run from the pens of the exegetes, for it is difficult to determine what, if anything, of importance

it adds to the first discourse. What is the point of the almost
baroque descriptions of the two great animals: the hippopotamus and Leviathan? Why this delight in description that seems
to detract from the dramatic climax which the book has now
reached?

The exegetes offer various answers. In my opinion, one of
the most relevant answers is that after speaking of nature, God
now speaks of history. That is, he uses the image of the two
beasts to refer to the two great powers which Israel regarded
as invincible and as capable of destroying the whole world:
Egypt, represented by the hippopotamus, a river animal, and
Mesopotamia, represented by Leviathan, a ferocious beast of
myth. God can look down even on these from a superior position and treat them playfully as it were, because he knows
them from within and, despite their cruelty, holds them in his
hand.

But whatever the meaning of the passage, God continues
his challenges to Job; he does not refer directly to what Job
has said but broadens the horizons to the limits of the possible
while calling upon this human being to exert his powers:

> Then the Lord answered Job out of the whirlwind:
> "Gird up your loins like a man;
>   I will question you, and you declare to me" (40:6-7).

Job is now extolled, even if somewhat ironically:

> Then I will also acknowledge to you
>   that your own right hand can give you victory (v. 14).

Some commentators observe that God has thus avoided
Job's problem, which was to know whether he was right or
wrong. The Lord tells him: You too are strong and I praise you,
but I too am right.

God's justice differs from ours; because of his mysterious
plan it is possible to glorify all three: God and the world and
the human person. This seems to be the meaning of God's
words.

After praising Job, God continues:

> Look at Behemoth,
>> which I made just as I made you;
>> it eats grass like an ox.
> Its strength is in its loins,
>> and its power in the muscles of its belly.
> It makes its tail stiff like a cedar;
>> the sinews of its thighs are knit together.
> Its bones are tubes of bronze,
>> its limbs like bars of iron (40:15-18).

And further on:

> Can you draw out Leviathan with a fishhook,
>> or press down its tongue with a cord?
> Can you put a rope in its nose,
>> or pierce its jaw with a hook? . . .
> Who can confront it and be safe?
>> —under the whole heaven, who?
> I will not keep silence concerning its limbs,
>> or its mighty strength, or its splendid frame. . . .
> On earth it has no equal,
>> a creature without fear.
> It surveys everything that is lofty;
>> it is king over all that are proud (41:1-34).

After God's lengthy description of the two beasts, Job replies:

> Then Job answered the Lord:
> "I know that you can do all things,
>> and that no purpose of yours can be thwarted.
> 'Who is this that hides counsel without knowledge?'
> Therefore I have uttered what I did not understand,
>> things too wonderful for me, which I did not know.
> 'Hear, and I will speak;
>> I will question you, and you declare to me.'
> I had heard of you by the hearing of the ear,
>> but my eye now sees you;
> therefore I despise myself,
>> and repent in dust and ashes" (42:1-6).

Job begins his response with a very beautiful statement which will be repeated, first by the angel to Mary and then by Jesus in reference to the rich young man and to the salvation of the wealthy: "Nothing is impossible for God." The divine plan is unfathomable; its truth lies beyond any possible evidence, whether material or moral. God is the Living One, the ultimate norm of love for the entire universe.

"Who is this that hides counsel without knowledge?" After contemplating the awesome mystery of Israel, St. Paul realizes that it must conceal an impenetrable plan, and he gives voice to the same certainty that Job had expressed (see Rom 11).

Job makes the ultimate act of obedience of the mind, which is also an act of praise: "Therefore I have uttered what I did not understand, things too wonderful for me, which I did not know" (42:3).

He thus passes judgment on what he himself had said: his words had contained an element of truth, but his discourse as a whole had been an effort to explore matters beyond his powers, matters that elude human beings.

Verse 5 represents, in my judgment, the supreme moment of the entire book, especially as far as its lesson for us is concerned:

> I had heard of you by the hearing of the ear,
>   but now my eye sees you.

Here we have the meaning of Job's long distress. He had known God from elementary instruction, from theology, from learned disquisitions, and from books. The knowledge thus communicated was evidently not false, but it was unable to unify reality, to bring the face of God into focus. As a result, Job lost his way as he tried to unify the multiplicity of arguments. Now his eyes have been illumined and he is able to see directly that human beings are not to speak about God; instead they are to listen to him and worship him.

When we put ourselves in this frame of mind—which I have been calling "affective," because it does not attempt to discover everything by the power of the intellect but rather submits to the mystery—we are given a connaturality with this mystery, a state which Jesus describes when he says: "Remain in me, and I in you." Then we can claim to see God with our eyes. Reasoning is obviously needed; theology and pastoral practice are needed; but the important thing, beyond all of these, is ultimate insight. This is the reason above all reasons, indeed the reason without reason, once we realize that in God there is only his being—his being for us, his being for me—and all reasons fall silent. Through submission to the mystery we acquire a true knowledge of Him from whom everything comes, to whom everything returns, and who unifies our existence.

We should note that God considers the arguments of Job to be better than those of his friends, who have limited themselves to a theological position that is very timid, overly prudent, overly tied to geometry rather than to profound theological truths. Job has ventured further; he has been more daring, more courageous, more passionate, and therefore he has drawn closer to the mystery of the Trinity, which is passionate self-giving, totality and gift. Nonetheless, because he has attempted to do this with words, he has remained still far off: "Therefore I despise myself, and repent in dust and ashes" (42:6).

He has at last attained to obedience of the mind, which consists of love, humility, loving reverence, and a submission that sums up the entire spirituality of the covenant: trust in him who has entered into covenant with me, surrender to him, no need of knowing everything about him or about myself, and therefore a deeper knowledge than can be acquired by subtle reasoning.

The Example of Jesus in Gethsemane

The third exemplar of obedience of the mind is Jesus in Gethsemane.

"They went to a place called Gethsemane; and he said to his disciples, 'Sit here while I pray.' He took with him Peter and James and John, and began to be distressed and agitated. And he said to them, 'I am deeply grieved, even to death; remain here, and keep awake.' And going a little farther, he threw himself on the ground and prayed that, if it were possible, the hour might pass from him' " (Mk 14:32-35).

We do not know whether this was the only deeply tragic moment of trial that Jesus experienced. There are hints elsewhere in the gospels that suggest it was not the only occasion; St. John, for example, speaks of profound perturbations and dangerous situations even during the public life.

Gethsemane is for us a quintessential instance of the temptations which the Letter to the Hebrews says marked the earthly life of Jesus: "We do not have a high priest who is unable to sympathize with our weaknesses, but we have one who in every respect has been tested as we are, yet without sin" (Heb 4:15).

"In every respect": therefore the fear, aversion, dreariness, disgust, and loss of motivation that we see surfacing in Gethsemane. This is the trial which we saw mentioned at the beginning of Hebrews 12.

What is the meaning of these feelings of anguish that climax in a sadness "even to death"?

It is not easy to enter by way of rational discourse into the setting of these feelings. We may perhaps be helped by affective prayer in which we try to become present to the consciousness of Jesus and to contemplate him by experiencing fear and anxiety along with him.

We can perhaps compare his fears with ours, especially with our fears for the reign of God and the burdens we do not know how to carry but which we feel weighing heavily upon us; fears for others and the serious spiritual dangers in which they live; fears caused by the failures or regressions of the Church; fears for the tragic situations of families and the sick and for the sufferings of young drug addicts; fears for the tragedies which mental illnesses cause in families, turning these into hells.

All these are in some degree a participation in the anguish and sadness which Jesus experienced.

Then, too, we are all familiar with the feelings of uselessness, disgust, desire for escape, and abandonment which these fears cause, for they are exemplified in the Book of Job.

The conditions under which Jesus lived are also summed up for us in the Letter to the Hebrews: "In the days of his flesh, Jesus offered up prayers and supplications, with loud cries and tears, to the one who was able to save him from death. . . . Although he was a Son, he learned obedience through what he suffered; and having been made perfect, he became the source of eternal salvation for all who obey him" (Heb 5:7-9). The emphasis here is on the idea of obedience: Jesus learned obedience of mind and became the source of salvation for those who learn to obey him.

How does Jesus respond in this struggle for obedience of the mind, a struggle in which many people flee, withdraw, and abandon everything?

He responds by *remaining*. He asks the disciples to remain and not to flee, not to change their situation but to face up to the struggle. Then, going a little farther, he throws himself on the ground and prays that if it be possible, this hour may pass from him.

How splendid that Jesus should not only face up to the evil but should do so with an admission of his own weakness, asking that "the hour might pass from him."

His struggle is with the Father, and he wants the Father's will to be victorious, no matter what the cost. Listen to him: "He said, 'Abba, Father, for you all things are possible; remove this cup from me; yet, not what I want, but what you want' " (Mk 14:36). He is aware of wanting a different outcome, of wanting the cup taken away from him, but his decisive words are "what you want."

These are the ultimate words of faith and obedience of the mind; they are the words that tell us the meaning of Abraham,

Job, and all the saints who travelled the way of faith in the Old Testament.

Let us continue in affective contemplation of Jesus in Gethsemane and keep asking him: What are you saying to me? How am I to live these situations?

Final Thoughts

I suggest three final thoughts:

1. If we are engaged in a struggle for obedience of the mind, *the model is Jesus in the Garden,* Jesus praying. He is the ultimate model who sums up in his person the whole struggle of Job with its violence and its victory. The best place for rereading the entire Book of Job and seeing how it opens up into the divine plan is alongside Jesus in Gethsemane.

2. *Those who pray* not to enter into temptation *have already won half the victory.* Jesus urges his apostles: "Pray that you may not enter into temptation," and he obliges us to repeat this petition over and over again in the Lord's Prayer. It is a petition the importance of which we do not always understand and which we often say with our lips only. In it we ask the Father that we may grasp the presence of struggle and trial in so many situations; that we may not rush headlong into them without realizing that they are trials but may confront them prayerfully. When we realize that a given situation or event is a trial to which God is subjecting us we have already half overcome the difficulty. On the other hand, when we interpret them as bad luck, as resulting from the iniquity of other people or society, or from the ignorance of superiors or the laziness of those entrusted to our care, then it is rather difficult to surmount such situations except by rational discourse or a program of measures which only partially solve the problem.

If I grasp the aspect of trial, I will cry out: "Lord, do not let me fall into temptation! Help me to understand that I am passing through an important moment of my life and that you are here with me, testing my faith and my love."

3. As Abraham, Job, and, above all, Jesus teach, true victory is found in *self-surrender* to the inexhaustible, creative, surprising mystery of God, who has means at his disposal that are beyond our ability to think and understand. We should never think that we are caught in a blind alley, for even when it seems that way to us, the Trinity is infinitely capable of rescuing us. Therefore the walls surrounding our existence, the blind alleys in which we feel trapped, are climbed and overcome by the self-surrender that is the supreme act of human freedom, the act in which human beings become most truly themselves, namely, creatures who are made for dialogue with God and who save themselves through a total reliance on him as a Father full of merciful love.

"Father, help us to know you in this way. Grant that our eyes may know and see you in an authentic way that reflects the truth of the kerygma and the gospel and leads to definitive salvation."

TWELVE

The Fulfillment of the Suffering Church

(Homily for the Feast of Saint Bartholomew)
(Readings: Revelation 21:9-14; 1 Corinthians 4:9-15;
and John 1:45-51)

The gospel describes a man who reminds us of Job. Nathanael is in fact an upright and honest man, a simple man who is all of a piece, a man capable of opening himself to the truth.

We read earlier: "The Lord said to Satan, 'Have you considered my servant Job? There is no one like him on the earth, a blameless and upright man who fears God and turns away from evil' " (Jb 1:8).

Now Jesus exclaims: "Here is truly an Israelite in whom there is no deceit!" (Jn 1:47).

Nathanael too is an upright man, nevertheless he will have to be tested.

His entire life will be a sharing in the mystery of the passion of Jesus, until he meets the supreme test: the martyrdom on which the Church has us meditate today.

The theme of the testing of apostles is extensively described by Paul: We, the apostles—those who are chosen, who have believed, who have let themselves be sent and agree that the justice of God should be made manifest in their persons—have been exhibited by God ''as last of all, as though sentenced to death, because we have become a spectacle to the world, to angels and to mortals.'' There are surprising words.

The phrase ''a spectacle to the world'' suggests the unequal fights in the amphitheater between men and wild beasts.

Paul goes on to use a series of negative terms: ''fools, weak, in disrepute, hungry, thirsty, poorly clothed, beaten, homeless, weary, reviled, persecuted, slandered, the rubbish of the world, the dregs of all things'' (vv. 9-13).

We are here reminded once again of Job, who drinks the cup to the last drop.

The mystery of the testing of the just becomes, in the passage of Paul, the mystery of the testing of apostles. The latter is suffused by a light, proper to the New Testament, which is only implicit in Job and breaks into the open only at the end of the book.

In Paul, the suffering is the same but there is a message to be read between the lines: the apostle who shares the lot of the suffering just man manifests the fulness of the resurrection: ''When reviled, we bless; when persecuted, we endure; when slandered, we speak kindly.''

Here can be seen the cross's splendid power.

All this brings us to the heavenly vision recorded in the first reading from the Book of Revelation. It can be read as a concluding vision in the Church's meditation on the Apostle Bartholomew. It is not an accident that all the liturgical prayers of this Mass focus on the theme of the Church.

When the Church thinks about St. Bartholomew, it thinks about its own mystery in the setting of the Apocalypse, where the Church is seen as persecuted and suffering, a Church that is the figure of Job writ large and yet at the same time looks forward to its own fulfillment.

The passage from the Apocalypse contains a very beautiful description of the messianic Jerusalem, which is given endearing names: ''the bride, the wife of the Lamb'' (21:9).

In the Eastern tradition these two names are equivalent, since the word *nymphē* (literally: "betrothed") means one who is definitively promised as a wife and is bound by a lifelong contract.

The two names are thus meant to signify the full marriage, the affective and indissoluble relationship, marked by equality, which God enters into with his people, and the trust which the people, the Church, have in God.

In the case of Job, this trust was still a troubled one; it had to toil to express itself.

In Mary of Nazareth and in the Canaanite woman the trust is voiced with all the rich love possible to a human heart: You cannot deceive me; I cannot but trust in you; you cannot fail to see the painful situation in which I am living, and you take it to heart because you have laid your hand upon me.

This is the Church that lives in the certainty of its being bride and wife of the Lamb, of him who holds the destinies of the universe in his hand and by his death has saved and redeemed history.

"And in the spirit he [the angel] carried me away to a great, high mountain and showed me the holy city Jerusalem coming down out of heaven from God. It has the glory of God" (21:10).

I have often asked myself why the Church is described in this way.

We imagine the contrary for ourselves: the Church advancing toward God through historical trials that purify it. The vision in the Apocalypse shows the Church in an unexpected way: as the Church that comes down from heaven.

What is the meaning of this somewhat paradoxical vision in relation to the ascending history which is our usual approach to the Church?

The meaning, it seems to me, is that while the Church is indeed a people journeying to its Lord, it is in its activity and accomplishments entirely a gift of God; it comes from on high, from grace, love, and mercy. Because it exists as a gift and because it is founded on Jesus, on the Lamb, it expresses the totality of salvation and true catholicity. In the Church there is an openness to all reality; in it are contained the Jewish people and the whole of humanity.

It is this vision of the Church that we pastors should always have before our eyes. We who see only fragmented parts, often imperfect, perhaps annoying, often inadequate, of the Church's fulfillment and who are tempted to frustration, loss of motivation, and loss of hope—we must feed ourselves on contemplation of this vision.

Sometimes, when celebrating a pontifical Mass or a Eucharist for a large crowd of people, I have been surprised by this vision, and I find myself in the presence of the wonderful work of God that comes down from on high.

My bodily eyes may see people who are distracted, drowsy, talkative, but with the gaze of faith I look with amazement on this bride, this wife, who thanks to the Eucharist comes down from the power of God and is being established in its definitive state.

This astonishment at the vision of Jerusalem coming down from on high helps us on our daily journey. It is a nourishment that continually restores us in the face of the unexpected disappointments we experience in the various particular incidents of our ministry.

"Lord, through the intercession of St. Bartholomew, grant us the clarity and certainty deriving from this vision of your work as one which comes down with utter sureness from on high and which you establish unqualifiedly and permanently in our world so full of uncertainty, fear, apprehension, and inconstancy.

"Grant that through this contemplation, especially as mediated by the Eucharist, the body and blood of your Son, we may be able to continue journeying and hoping, because we gaze on the invisible that is already present: the Church of God which comes down from on high to gladden the earth with its proclamation of definitive salvation."

THIRTEEN

Job and the Song of Songs

The Ineffable Mystery of the Trinity

It is with some apprehension that I take up the subject of this final meditation: Job and the Song of Songs. This is because I am entering into areas of adoration of the mystery that belong to the mystical sphere, of which it is always better to be silent than to speak.

Nonetheless the events of our lives, our trials, the multitude of pressures brought to bear on us from within and from without all impel us to seek contact with the Trinitarian mystery in which the human race, the world, and history have their roots.

• I shall begin by reading to you a provocative passage from a recent article of David Maria Turoldo, in which he reflects on the incurable illness from which he is suffering. He asks himself whether it is right that he should pray to be healed of the illness and saved from death. He skims through the gospel, which in his opinion is very reserved on the subject, and calls attention to the incidents that speak in favor of such prayer (the blind man asks for sight; the centurion's servant asks mercy for his master's daughter; Lazarus is restored to

life; the Canaanite woman pleads and wins her suit). ''But,''
he continues,

> the problem takes on its full dimensions in relation to God him-
> self. No, I do not think it right for me to pray that God would
> heal me. I can understand such a prayer, but only at the human
> level, at the level of a Job who is still groping in the darkness
> of his suffering and despair; in other words, I can accept such
> a prayer as a necessary outlet for and way out of anguish.
>
> I do not pray God to intervene; I pray that he will give me
> the strength to endure the suffering and to face death with the
> courage of Christ. I do not pray for God to change; I pray in
> order to be filled with God and for a possible change in myself,
> that is, in us, all of us together, and in things (D. M. Turoldo,
> ''Cosa pensare e come pregare di fronte al male,'' *Servitium*
> [1989], no. 64).

This passage demands that we attend to certain aspects of
the mystery that we would not otherwise dare to confront.

• The same attention is demanded, above all, by not a few
statements of Jesus, beginning with the predictions of his passion. ''Then he began to teach them that the Son of Man must
undergo great suffering, and be rejected by the elders, the chief
priests, and the scribes, and be killed, and after three days rise
again. He said all this quite openly'' (Mk 8:31-32a).

This statement is repeated three times. It can be said that
we know of no other historical personage who during his life
spoke so much of his death as Jesus did, and who even inter-
preted his life in terms of his death and thus acted in view of
his death.

The prophecies of the passion, which the gospels unfail-
ingly record, are confirmed by other statements. For example:
''I came to bring fire to the earth, and how I wish it were already kindled! I have a baptism with which to be baptized,
and what stress I am under until it is completed!'' (Lk 12:49-50).
I think also of psalm verses which spiritual writers have ap-

plied to the incarnation of the Word and to his commitment to the struggle against sin:

> In the heavens he has set a tent for the sun,
>> which comes out like a bridegroom from his
>>> wedding canopy,
>> and like a strong man runs its course with joy (Ps 19:4-5).

The impression is given to us that Jesus desires trials and faces them joyfully.

The psalmist continues:

> Its rising is from the end of the heavens,
>> and its circuit to the end of them;
>> and nothing is hidden from its heat (v. 6).

Jesus says again, at the beginning of the Last Supper: "I have eagerly desired to eat this Passover with you before I suffer" (Lk 22:15). The same desire to fling himself into trials can also be seen in the symbolic gesture of washing his disciples' feet: "Jesus knew that his hour had come to depart from this world and go to the Father. Having loved his own who were in the world, he loved them to the end."

He then rose from table, set aside his garments, took a towel and girded himself with it, poured water, and washed the disciples' feet. This he did to signify that he gives his life for us, for the sake of our life, in order to cleanse us. Did he not say to Peter: "Unless I wash you, you have no share with me" (Jn 13:1-8).

Let us try, therefore, to enter into the consciousness of Jesus. This consciousness is, on the one hand, the exemplar for all humankind, since Jesus is the head of the redeemed human race, the first-born from the dead, the first-born of creation, the one in whom we discover our vocation as creatures and human beings, since we have been created and re-created in him. On the other hand, this consciousness allows us to contemplate, in Jesus, the mystery of the Trinity, of God's own interior life.

Two Unwearying Quests

With the preceding as a background let us reflect on the relationship between Job and the Song of Songs.

At first sight there would seem to be no connection at all, since the two books are so different from one another. But they have in common at least the fact that both of them describe in detail an unwearying search.

Job's unwearying search is for divine justice, for the way in which this justice manifests itself and by means of which human beings can understand it. The Song of Songs describes an unwearying search for love, for the face and presence of the beloved, and for the joy this presence brings.

1. Job gropes his way; he is like a blind man moving through darkness, and yet in the midst of his suffering some flashes of light appear. One such flash, the subject of extensive exegetical commentary but, like the entire book, very difficult to interpret, comes toward the end of Chapter 19:

> Have pity on me, have pity on me, O you my friends,
>> for the hand of God has touched me!
> Why do you, like God, pursue me,
>> never satisfied with my flesh
> O that my words were written down!
>> O that they were inscribed in a book!
> O that with an iron pen and with lead
>> they were engraved on a rock forever!
> For I know that my Redeemer lives,
>> and that at the last he will stand upon the earth;
> and after my skin has been thus destroyed,
>> then in my flesh I shall see God,
> whom I shall see on my side [or: for myself],
>> and my eyes shall behold, and not another (Jb 19:21-27).

These are enigmatic words, and the interpreters translate them in different ways. All the interpreters agree, however, that the words point to a flash of certainty and trust which transcends all that has gone before, because it is based on something beyond human insight.

2. Comparable flashes of light and impetuous searches are to be seen in the Song of Songs.

I shall cite chiefly passages from the sections to which *The New Jerusalem Bible* gives the titles "Second Poem" and "Fourth Poem."

• The bride speaks:

> The voice of my beloved!
>> Look, he comes,
> leaping upon the mountains,
>> bounding over the hills.
> My beloved is like a gazelle
>> or young stag.
> Look, there he stands
>> behind our wall.
> gazing in at the windows,
>> looking through the lattice.
> My beloved speaks and says to me:
> "Arise, my love, my fair one,
>> and come away;
> For now the winter is past,
>> the rain is over and gone.
> The flowers appear on the earth;
>> the time of singing has come,
> and the voice of the turtledove
>> is heard in our land.
> The fig tree puts forth its figs,
>> and the vines are in blossom;
>> they give forth fragrance.
> Arise, my love, my fair one,
>> and come away.
> O my dove, in the clefts of the rock,
>> in the covert of the cliff,
> let me see your face,
>> let me hear your voice;
> for your voice is sweet,
>> and your face is lovely (Cant 2:8-14).

In the end, this cry and these words remain an unfulfilled desire:

> Upon my bed at night
> I sought him whom my soul loves;
> I sought him, but found him not (3:1).

The longing that is so characteristic of the search in the Book of Job is also expressed in the Song, but so is the disappointment. Yet the bride does not admit she is defeated; she does not give up, because her search is inspired by love and not by rational, logical considerations.

Indeed, she continues to search even after she has failed to find:

> "I will rise now and go about the city,
> in the streets and in the squares;
> I will seek him whom my soul loves."
> I sought him, but found him not.
> The sentinels found me,
> as they went about the city.
> "Have you seen him whom my soul loves?"
> Scarcely had I passed them,
> when I found him whom my soul loves.
> I held him, and would not let him go
> until I brought him into my mother's house,
> and into the chamber of her that conceived me (3:2-4).

What is described here is an ongoing game: the beloved comes and calls, but there is no meeting; then he is appealed to and flees, but in the end is found and held.

• The fourth poem surprises us because the beloved is once again distant and still being sought:

> Listen! my beloved is knocking.
> "Open to me, my sister, my love,
> my dove, my perfect one;
> for my head is wet with dew,
> my locks with the drops of the night."

> I had put off my garment;
>> how could I put it on again?
> I had bathed my feet;
>> how could I soil them?
> My beloved thrust his hand into the opening,
>> and my inmost being yearned for him.
> I arose to open to my beloved,
>> and my hands dripped with myrrh,
> my fingers with liquid myrrh,
>> upon the handles of the bolt.
> I opened to my beloved,
>> but my beloved had turned and was gone.
> My soul failed me when he spoke.
> I sought him, but did not find him;
>> I called him, but he gave no answer (5:2-6).

Now begins a lengthy dialogue, first with the sentinels, and then with the chorus; this time it seems that the bride does not succeed in finding her beloved.

Throughout the Song, the basic theme is repeated between dialogues: "My beloved is mine, and I am his." These are words of trust and are uttered only in the absence of the beloved. Like everything that is important in the Bible, they are spoken three times: "My beloved is mine, and I am his" (2:16); "I am my beloved's and my beloved is mine" (6:3); "I am my beloved's, and his desire is for me" (7:10).

So too: you are my God, we are your people; you are my people, I am your God. How can we fail to see that the words of the Song recast the covenant formula in terms of reciprocal intimacy?

An indestructible covenant, unlimited trust, expectation, astonishment, utter certainty, even though the beloved is not there, even if we are searching for him, even if we do not yet possess him.

In the Song of Songs, then, we have the theme of a search based on the indestructible hope that he whom we seek is there and loves us and that we shall find him; at the same time, there is the theme of the anxiety, suffering, and expectation produced by the search. The finding produces surprise, joy, peace, and enthusiasm; this is immediately followed by a new loss and therefore longing, petition, and supplication.

The Song gives the impression of describing the game of love which, in its simplest forms, is found everywhere in human life: from its elementary manifestation in the mother who hides herself from her child in order to let it experience the enthusiastic joy of finding her again, to the experience of authentic friendship. Love desires both absence and presence, hiddenness and the search that increases surprise and joy.

I have been struck by some pages of Adrienne von Speyr. This modern mystic reflects on the theme of the game of love as seen in every relationship—friend, marriage, family, and so on—and then applies it to the mystery of the Trinity. This last she understands to be a mystery of loving relationships in which something similar to the game of love can be seen, for in the Trinity love is never flat or stale but enchanting, creative, dynamic, and enthusiastic. I think this to be a very careful and profound observation, once we stop reducing the interior mystery of God to a motionless ocean and understand it instead to be full of the vigor, the enjoyment of the unpredictable and of adventure, the unceasing dynamism, which alone can explain creation and the risk God has taken of having a partner with whom to dialogue. God risks the possibility of rejection because he wants the possibility of entering into a dialogue of authentic love. We can understand in the same light the Son's desire to embark on the human adventure, to accept trials and face them from within, so that in his relationships with human beings as with the Father, he may bring into existence a rich love that is never wearied, never extinguished.

A God Who Hides Himself

We can now understand better the significance of ''mystical'' trials, which are among the most terrible anyone can face:

the night of the senses, the night of the spirit, the night of faith
in which human beings grope their way in a state of almost
total despair because of the absence of that total love without
which they can no longer live. In these mysterious movements
of the spirit we see something enabling us to understand how,
against the background of the mystery of God, they can have
a very specific meaning which is grasped not by purely logical
argument but by way of sympathy with the divine. God hides
himself so that he may be sought and found; the search for
him, even if profoundly painful, is part of the game of love,
a necessary passage to a truer experience. The words, "I
sought, but I did not find," thus highlight a powerful element
in the dynamics of our knowledge of God.

When all is said and done, Job too can say: I sought but
I did not find, since he did not receive the answer he wanted
to trap God into making. But he does reach the point of saying: "Now my eyes see you," whereas previously "I had heard
of you by the hearing of the ear" (Jb 42:5), for now I have
entered more deeply into your mystery.

If the grace has been given to us of experiencing times of
darkness and suffering, searching and loving, or sharing the
experience of others who pass through such times, we can perhaps glimpse something more of the mystery of night and trial,
even if we cannot express it in logical terms. This mystery is
not bound by the strict laws of justice—"Who sinned, this man
or his parents, that he was born blind?"—but has its place
within the mystery revealed by Jesus: "so that God's works
might be revealed in him" (Jn 9:2-3).

Since God is a mystery of surprise-filled and ever-active
relationality, he communicates himself through the dynamism
of a search made up of shadows and lights, concealments and
manifestations. Not therefore through logical, crystalline, carte-
sian clarity, such as human beings would always like to have.
Not as the brothers of Jesus would like when they urge him
to show himself. Jesus does show himself, but after the manner of the mystery of God, that is, by becoming present and

hiding himself. He manifests himself in his miracles and hides himself in the humiliation of the cross; he manifests himself in the resurrection, but only to some close friends, and he hides himself as regards the spectacular displays which his world and the world in every age look for from him.

It would certainly be easier for us to believe in a God who uses the stage of history for a great fireworks display.

But the God of revelation is by his nature mysterious; he does not engage in trite, ostentatious self-display, but requires searching, playing, and continually renewed relationships.

If, then, we are to know this God, we must seek him and take part in his game. Those who try to reduce him to a dialectical scheme different from the one he follows will have trouble knowing and accepting him. They will accept him with their intellects but will not resign themselves to the fact that he is not what they expect him to be. We must enter into the game and "rejoice like strong men" that we can run this road, as the sun runs it from one end of the earth to the other. The game is always serious because it involves a risk, but it is also lighthearted and joyous. I think here of the ascent of a mountain face: this too is undertaken for fun and not after calculating its utility. Its doing therefore brings pleasure; people even do it because it is risky, because they are afraid not to do it. But as they overcome the various difficulties and begin to glimpse the summit, they feel the sudden joy of having conquered, a joy impossible to those who reach the top in the comfort of a chair-lift.

When we understand all this we are beginning to have a true knowledge of God. Knowledge "by the hearing of the ear" has its weaknesses. We can indeed know God in his imaginative, playful, surprising, creative relationships, we can know him as a Trinity of love, but only if we run the climber's risk as we try to become like the Son of God who came to play in the created universe to the point of giving it life.

Job, a Poem of Love

As I come to the end of this retreat and of my reflections on the Book of Job, I have to say that even the problem of Job is a problem of love: a love which, in this case, feels rejected, yet believes against all appearances; a love that lashes out and cries and screams and suffers because it wants to remove the veils from the object loved.

In the introductory meditation on the mystery of trials I spoke of Satan's wager regarding human beings: that a completely selfless love is not to be found in them nor an authentic freedom capable of self-surrender.

I do not know whether or not my love of God is truly selfless, and if I claimed to know it I would find myself in Job's difficulties and would be afflicted with endless anxiety.

I do know, however, that God tries me and that by his own mysterious paths he will bring my love to the point of complete purification. The problem of pure, selfless love is not my problem; it is the problem of the God who has confidence in me and knows me to be capable of a love equal to his own.

It is for me to give God my whole self, along with all the wealth of satisfactions, human and divine, that the Lord allows me to experience.

It is for him to draw me to himself in the way he regards as truest and most authentic.

For the rest—and the Song of Songs gives us this insight—true love is its own fulfillment, its own beauty, its own wealth, its own reward. It is when we grasp this that we enter into the love of God, that love which has its justification only in itself.

Such are the horizons that we have glimpsed and that every lover knows. Lovers know perfectly well that love is freely given, even if it then feeds on countless satisfactions. But in its innermost essence it is an unrivaled gift of self and thus a reflection of the life of the Trinity.

Let us ask the Lord to increase our understanding of our experiences so that we may overcome a little our ignorance of him and hear Jesus say to us: "You have stood by me in my trials," now you know me better and are ready to reign with me because you have suffered with me.

As the tenth anniversary of my episcopal service approaches, I myself feel the need of telling you and all the priests of the diocese how very grateful I am that you have stood by me in my trials; that you have followed your bishop faithfully on his way of trials by carrying your own crosses courageously and spiritedly.

"Lord, our trials are yours and yours are ours. As we meditate on your blessed passion, we desire to enter into the koinonia, *the fellowship, with your sufferings that will make us certain of experiencing the power of your resurrection."*

Let us pray that we may complete this exacting but wonderful journey.

FOURTEEN

A Luminous Example of Selfless Love

(Homily for Friday of the Twentieth Week of Ordinary Time)
(Readings: Ruth 1:3-8, 14-16, 22; Matthew 22:34-40)

Today we begin to read the Book of Ruth in the weekday liturgy. The story is a peaceful interlude in the picture of bloodshed, wars, struggles, conflicts, cruelties, and infidelities that is given to us in the Book of Judges.

The story of Ruth shows that even in periods in which human beings seem to turn into "wolves" preying on others and in which they seem reduced to dealing with one another as wild animals, there are episodes displaying love, charity, kindness, and selfless behavior. This is, then, a very beautiful little book, set like a precious stone in the grim picture of Israel's feudal period.

It is beautiful for another reason: it tells of the grandmother of David and therefore an ancestress of the Messiah. Bethlehem, the city in which Jesus will be born, is also mentioned. Everything in the story gives a foretaste of the intimacy, tenderness, and joy of Christmas.

The story begins by describing a great social, political, and cultural trial: a famine and resultant emigration, with all the sufferings inflicted on those who are forced to go off to distant lands. Many Italians experienced this suffering at one time; today it is felt by others who at last reach our country and indeed all the countries of Europe. Tomorrow I shall be traveling to Frankfurt for a gathering with that city on the occasion of a centenary of the cathedral. I shall have to give a report on the theme of the new multiracial European civilization that is now coming into existence due to the mass immigrations from the Third World. In Germany alone it is estimated that there are more than five million immigrants, the majority of them Turks.

Thus the suffering of emigrants is still a worldwide phenomenon today. It is a tremendous trial for human beings to be uprooted from their native land and those dear to them, and have to face insecurity.

The Book of Ruth describes this trial, which is exacerbated by a very painful family trial: Elimelech, husband of Naomi, dies and later her two sons as well. Hers is a family pursued by misfortune, almost (one might say) a family which God has forgotten. Naomi has lost everything; she lacks hope and a future. Then, in a heroic and selfless gesture, she urges her two Moabite daughters-in-law to save themselves by returning to their homes and leaving her to die in her grief. She wants what is best for the two women. It is in this situation that Ruth's courage shows most clearly, for she is a Moabite and therefore a foreigner to Israel and in addition a member of a people hated by the Israelites. Moab is a symbol of a people rejected; the psalmist says, "Moab is my washbasin" (Ps 108:9). Yet from this people comes Ruth, a powerful and luminous example of pure, authentic, selfless love.

Ruth answers Naomi:

> "Do not press me to leave
> or to turn back from following you!
> Where you go, I will go;
> Where you lodge, I will lodge;
> Your people shall be my people,
> and your God my God.

> Where you die, I will die—
>> there will I be buried. . . ."

> So Naomi returned together with Ruth the Moabite, her daughter-in-law, who came back with her from the country of Moab. They came to Bethlehem at the beginning of the barley harvest (Ruth 1:16-17, 22).

When we view Ruth's behavior in the context of the power exerted by family traditions such as are still very much alive today among, for example, the peoples of Africa, we are surprised by the simplicity with which she gives up a whole system of relationships and chooses to go with her mother-in-law to a people which is not her own, which she does not know, and to which her only tie is her husband, now dead and unable to protect her. In order to remain with Naomi she chooses insecurity, loneliness, and possibly contempt.

Her action is entirely selfless; it has no reasons to support it. The logical thing for her was to return to her own home, make a new life for herself there, and forget about any venture with this foreign Israelite woman. Instead, urged on by an interior force, she faces the unknown and remains faithful to the memory of her husband and to his mother. "Where you go, I will go; Where you lodge I will lodge; your people shall be my people, and your God my God." We hear an echo of the covenant formula: You shall be my people, and I will be your God.

Ruth is drawn by the mystery of the covenant and enters into it lovingly, joyously, trustingly. The continuation of the story will show that this self-surrender makes her a new, creative, passionate woman. Emerging from the straitjacket of traditions that would have confined her in a narrow role within her clan, she accepts the game of love that is offered to her, the new mystery of which she knows little but which she finds wonderfully attractive.

Because of her wonderful story and her subsequent happy marriage to Boaz, this woman will have a place in the genealogy of Christ. Every time we read the beginning of Matthew's gospel we remember her, her fidelity, her illogical love that in the end is fully justified.

We have meditated at length during this retreat on the mystery of trials and love. Let us now ask once again, here before the image of the Mother of Sorrows, that we may enter more deeply into this mystery.

Let us pray a good deal for one another, now and in the days ahead, and ask with longing that the selfless love which is a fruit given by the Spirit alone may be given to us in abundance through the intercession of Mary and all the saints.

Index of Biblical References